"A good performance appraisal can provide detailed instructions on how your employees can overcome problems, improve, and grow. That's why a performance appraisal should not be viewed as an end in itself, but as an ongoing management process that should start the minute your employees begin their jobs or the day you take the job as their manager.**"**

While Barnes & Noble and the author have used best efforts in writing this book, they make no representations or warranties as to its accuracy and completeness. It is sold with the understanding that neither the author nor Barnes & Noble is engaged in rendering legal, accounting, or other professional service. If legal advice or other expert assistance is required, the services of a competent professional person should be sought.

FIRST EDITION

2004 Barnes & Noble Books   .

Barnes & Noble Publishing
122 Fifth Avenue
New York, NY 10011

ISBN 0760746915

2 4 6 8 10 9 7 5 3 1

Printed and bound in the United States of America

BARNES & NOBLE

MANAGEMENT
BASICS™

PERFORMANCE APPRAISALS

CATHY LEE GIBSON

**BARNES
& NOBLE
BOOKS**

NEW YORK

Foreword

I t's that time of year again: performance appraisal time. Your anxiety is starting to build. Here's a secret of top managers: If you approach the appraisal process as an opportunity to communicate with employees about their goals, it can help improve their performance and morale.

How do you do this? That's where Barnes & Noble Management Basics' *Performance Appraisals* comes in. This clearly written, step-by-step manager's guide shows you how to set up an effective system for documenting employees' performance year-round. Once your system is in place, you'll get expert advice on setting realistic, measurable goals with employees, as well as tips on monitoring employees' progress and providing constructive feedback. You'll also learn how to avoid many of the common errors managers make, such as confusing personality with performance and comparing employees with each other.

But best of all, *Performance Appraisals* gives you over 200 sample phrases you can use when writing about key job abilities—from problem-solving skills to dependability.

So start reading and see just how easy it is to turn performance appraisals into a handy management tool that not only encourages your employees' success but yours as well.

Wynn Madrigal
Editorial Director
Barnes & Noble Management Basics™ series

TABLE
OF CONTENTS

CHAPTER ONE

PERFORMANCE APPRAISAL BASICS

The appraisal opportunity

Your tool for communicating with and motivating employees

Okay, it's performance appraisal time. This is good news. How so, you ask incredulously? Because giving feedback to your **direct reports** about their performance is essential to their success . . . and yours. In other words, you can't succeed unless they do. Done right, performance appraisals can pinpoint exactly where your employees are on the success grid. Consider the performance appraisal a wonderful opportunity not only to expand your management skills, but also to familiarize yourself with each job and each employee you manage. Yes, that does involve taking stock of your employees, which means making assessments. Again, that is a good thing because often it is only in the process of doing a performance appraisal that problems are truly addressed and, better still, solved. In some cases, a **performance appraisal meeting** can even turn around an employee's career.

Your first step involves familiarizing yourself with the performance appraisal system and forms already in place at your company. Start by contacting your company's human resources department. They can provide you with the appraisal forms as well as guidance on how to fill them out. They can also provide you with some much-needed background information about your employees, namely their job descriptions (see pages 14) and their previous performance appraisals.

NOTE: If your company doesn't have a system or forms in place, then ask your HR department to recommend one that you can use.

WHERE DID PERFORMANCE APPRAISALS COME FROM?

Prior to World War II, performance appraisals were used only in the military. But that changed in 1954 when the management guru Peter Drucker came up with the idea of managing by objectives, or MBO. Instead of focusing on the day-to-day "activity trap" of the job, Drucker suggested managers keep their eye on long-term objectives and find ways to measure how well their workers were meeting them. One way to measure whether a company's goals were being met was to evaluate performance and give feedback. But just how should that feedback be given? Enter management theory X and Y by Douglas McGregor. This theory holds that there are two kinds of managers, those who feel that workers need to be coerced and controlled in order to do their jobs (theory X) and those who believe that employees want to learn and achieve on the job and need only to be guided in the right direction (theory Y).

The first performance appraisals were created by putting together MBO and theory Y. In essence, if managers sat down with their employees and mutually set goals and objectives and then reviewed their success, this not only empowered their employees, but also increased productivity! In the 1960s, General Electric demonstrated the effectiveness of performance appraisals, provided managers focused on their employees' attaining mutually agreed-upon goals. Salary and promotions were not to enter into the performance discussion.

Since then, the once-a-year performance appraisal has evolved into a performance management system that feeds back into a company's short- and long-term objectives. Smart managers use performance management to anchor their management styles. Done right, performance management can help you motivate your star workers to work even better, encourage poor performers without demoralizing them, find out who needs training before the lack of it becomes a detriment, and help objectively determine who should be promoted and who should be let go.

The appraisal timeline

Know your dates, then give yourself plenty of time

A good performance appraisal can provide detailed instructions on how your employees can overcome problems, improve, and grow. That's why a performance appraisal should not be viewed as an end in itself, but as an ongoing management process that should start the minute your employees begin their jobs or the day you take the job as their manager. You want to maximize the time you have to evaluate the performance of your direct reports.

That measurement period needs to have a beginning and an end—typically a year. (This time is called the **performance measurement period**.) When does this period of time officially start? Some organizations schedule performance appraisals to take place on the anniversary of an employee's hire date—this is called an **anniversary date** system. (For transferred employees, the anniversary is their transfer start date; for newly promoted employees, it is their promotion start date.) Some companies set one time for all performance appraisals to be done, regardless of hire or start date—this is called a **common review** or focal-point review system.

Once you know this date, you can plan your performance appraisal timeline. This means allotting enough time to make sure you can do a thorough job of evaluating an employee's performance.

APPRAISAL TIMELINE

There are seven key steps in the performance appraisal process. To make this a little easier to get your mind around, divide these seven steps into two sections.

The first section includes Steps 1, 2, and 3, which are activities that managers do on an ongoing basis throughout the year.

Step 1: Set performance goals and review regularly
Step 2: Create development plan and review regularly
Step 3: Provide regular feedback

The second section—Steps 4, 5, 6, and 7—focuses on what you need to do as you approach the end of the performance measurement period. This part usually takes about four to six weeks to complete.

Step 4: Write first draft of employee's appraisal
Step 5: Review employee's completed self-appraisal
Step 6: Reconcile differences and write final draft
Step 7: Schedule and hold performance appraisal meeting

Using the job description

Before you even start thinking about the performance appraisal process, take a look at each of your employees' job descriptions. A well-written **job description** supports the performance appraisal process in several ways. First, the responsibilities and tasks are one important source of information from which to develop individual employee goals. This section may include quantitative or qualitative **objectives** against which an employee's performance can be measured. Finally, the minimum requirements/qualifications section of the job description can help identify desired **skills**, areas of **knowledge**, and behavioral characteristics, which can then be compared to the employee's performance.

Although job descriptions vary from organization to organization, common elements include:

- Organization Name
- Department Name
- Job Title
- Supervisor's Job Title
- Overall Purpose/Objective of the Job
- Major Responsibilities/Duties/Tasks
- Minimum Requirements/Qualifications
- Date Prepared
- Preparer's Name

Assuming the job description summarizes the responsibilities and **outputs** of a particular job, it can be compared to an employee's performance throughout the appraisal period.

NOTE: If you don't have job descriptions, ask HR for help or conduct **job analysis** to create these vital documents following the format described here.

WHAT A JOB DESCRIPTION SHOULD COVER

A thorough job description should consist of much more than just a line that states "other duties as assigned." Take a closer look:

Requirements/Qualifications: Many employers indicate how many years of related experience or education are required to perform a particular job. Good job descriptions go beyond this part by outlining the specific skills, areas of knowledge, and behavioral characteristics required.

Skills: These are the specific abilities the employee must possess in order to perform the job successfully. Well-written descriptions of skills begin with the words "the ability to." Example: "The ability to understand and carry out written instructions."

Areas of Knowledge: This refers to specific expertise that the employee needs to have to perform the job. An example would be "knowledge of cosmetology."

Responsibilities/Tasks: These are the primary duties that an employee in this position is expected to carry out. Duties often make up the bulk of a job description, although it's impossible to provide a full list of every task an employee will have to perform. Because of this, many employers add the phrase "other duties as assigned." If you do this, just make sure that you've covered the essential job functions in detail.

Behavioral Characteristics: These are the traits that the successful employee will need to demonstrate while performing this job. They are defined in terms of actual, observable behaviors and outline specifically what it takes for someone to function effectively within the organization and to perform the job well. Make these descriptions detailed and use active verbs to make them come alive. For example, instead of simply saying that a receptionist must be "friendly," a more useful description would be "interact effectively with visitors," or perhaps, "create a welcoming environment in the reception area."

What's in the form?

There are many types of performance appraisal forms in use—in fact, there are probably as many different forms as there are organizations. It's smart to familiarize yourself with your company's form before you get into the details. Here is an overview of the standard categories:

A. Goals or Objectives These are projects, tasks, or assignments that the employee is expected to accomplish during the performance measurement period. They may relate to ongoing responsibilities that are a regular part of the job. They may be based on particular assignments or special projects that must be completed during this period, or they may be a combination of these two kinds of goals.

B. Competencies These are the skills or abilities, such as typing or project management, that employees need to demonstrate in order to perform their jobs successfully. Some organizations identify one set of competencies for all of their employees. Others require different competencies for different groups of employees (managers, technical employees, etc.). Often, examples of representative behaviors for each competency are included to ensure that the appraisal remains focused on behaviors—and not on personality or attitude.

C. Values This refers to what matters most to the organization, its mission or philosophy, and how the employees embody this. Values define what kind of behavior is acceptable—and what kind is unacceptable. For instance, one value might be "integrity," and an example of behaving with integrity might be refusing a gift from a client seeking to do business with you.

D. Development Plan This part of the form may focus on two different areas. First, it may identify skills or competencies that the employee needs to develop in order to perform his or her current job better. Second, it may talk about ways the employee can develop in order to grow within his or her chosen field or within the organization.

PERFORMANCE APPRAISAL FORM

Employee: _____ Title: _____
Department: _____
Supervisor: _____
Hire Date: _____ Appraisal date: _____

SECTION 1: GOALS AND OBJECTIVES

Goal   Rating (1–5):   Comments
_____   _____   _____
_____   _____   _____
_____   _____   _____
_____   _____   _____

Overall Rating:_____

SECTION 2 : COMPETENCIES (5 = far exceeds expectations)

Skill   Rating (1–5):   Comments
_____   _____   _____
_____   _____   _____
_____   _____   _____
_____   _____   _____

Overall Rating:_____

SECTION 3: VALUES

Key values: _____

Comments: _____

Rating (1–5): _____

SECTION 4: DEVELOPMENT PLAN

Development goal   By target date
_____   _____
_____   _____

_____   _____
Employee signature   Manager signature

The goals section

The goals section is the heart of the performance appraisal form and really serves as the motor that drives employee performance. It sets the goalposts for employee behavior and provides managers with a basis for evaluating performance at the end of the year. **Goals** describe *what* must be accomplished in the job.

How these goals are defined varies by organization. Some organizations require managers to define an employee's individual performance goals to reflect most (or even all) of the key required outputs listed in the job description. Conversely, other organizations require individual performance goals to be defined in terms of special projects that go above and beyond the requirements of the job.

Some forms list the department or organization's mission before the individual performance goals to encourage employees to link their own goals to the bigger ones.

Sometimes "subgoals," or benchmarks, that employees are supposed to reach along the way are also included. These may have target dates attached, or they may not. Other forms just require that the overall goals be listed, which puts emphasis on whether these goals are achieved, rather than on the steps followed to reach them.

On many forms, managers must rate employees on how well they fulfilled these goals using descriptive phrases or a weighted system (for more on ratings systems, see page 24). When goals are set, it's important for managers and employees to make sure they are on the same wavelength when it comes to expectations and what is considered "acceptable" performance so there are no end-of-the-year surprises.

Any way you slice it, this section of the appraisal form—because it is so critical—should be filled out with care.

GOALS SECTION

Employee Name: Erik Meyers
Title: Assistant Sales Manager
Dept: Corporate Sales
Appraisal Date: April 2004

GOALS AND OBJECTIVES - FY 2003

GOAL #1:
Generate $1 million worth of new business from no more than five new clients by end of FY 2003.
Results: Generated $1.2 million of business from four new clients by end of FY 2003, as well as an additional $200,000 from an existing client.
Rating: Exceeded expectations.

GOAL #2:
Conduct survey of top 50 corporate sales clients to assess satisfaction level by April 2003; tabulate, analyze, and present results at national sales conference in November 2003.
Results: Finished survey in April 2003. Presented brief at national sales conference, generating much positive feedback from colleagues.
Rating: Met expectations.

GOAL #3:
Perform due diligence for all new contracts. Conduct financial review, site visits, and provide support for new clients. Not to exceed contract error rate of 2% and customer complaint level of 5%.
Results: Began the year by working closely with contracts team to sign his new clients, but lost some momentum during the second half of the year, resulting in a total error rate of 3%. Customer complaint level is currently 10%. Needs to initiate more frequent site visits.
Rating: Did not fully meet expectations.

The competencies section

This section of the form can vary greatly, depending on both the company and the job's complexity. It can include specific examples of skills, like typing or using a particular software program, that the employee displayed during the appraisal period. Or it can include general descriptions or categories of ability without much detail or clarification. **Competencies** describe *how* goals or objectives are to be met.

Some forms require managers to provide specific examples of occasions on which employees have demonstrated each competency, while other forms simply require the manager to rate the employee's general skill level. Still other forms require the manager to make comments only if the employee performed above or below a certain level.

Competencies listed on the form can vary by individual employee, category of employee (such as managers and nonmanagers), department—or any combination of these. Other forms require all employees to be evaluated on exactly the same competencies. As with goals, on some forms competencies may be weighted, with certain ones being more important than others.

SAMPLE

COMPETENCY SECTION

Name: Cynthia B.

Position: Elementary School Teacher (Grade 2)

Rating scale: 1–5 (1=poor, 5=far exceeds expectations)

Competency	Rating	Comments
Management	4	Class is always well-behaved.
Problem-solving	3	Solves problems quickly and effectively.
Leadership	5	Encourages initiative and participation.
Resourcefulness	3	Makes good use of limited space and supplies.
Knowledge	4	Has particularly strong math skills.
Communication	2	Slower students need more attention.

VALUES SECTION

Some forms—but not all—require managers to evaluate how well the employee demonstrated the values of the organization, or lived up to the company's ideals.

If a form does incorporate values, they may simply be listed at the top of the first page as a point of reference. Alternatively, an entire section may be devoted to detailing specific examples of when and how the employee supported the organization's set of values. In most cases, individual values are not weighted (assigned a score based on how important they are; see page 24). If the values are rated, however, they will often be weighted less heavily than competencies or performance goals, or constitute a smaller percentage of the overall rating.

SAMPLE VALUES SECTION
Name: Vicki Ellis
Title: Support Specialist, Wholesale Dept.

CORE VALUES
Support of company mission
- Actions and standards reflect mission to be top organic-produce supplier on West Coast.
- Performance reflects commitment to outstanding customer service.

Commitment to superior value
- Acts speedily and effectively to correct client complaints.
- Stays informed of competitive developments.

Integrity
- Conducts self in responsible manner at all times.
- Upholds standards of honesty and fairness in all situations.

OVERALL RATING
Performance is above standard.

The development plan

Looking toward the future

Some appraisal forms have a concluding section on employee development—considered an important tool by many management experts. The suggestions for employee training or skill enhancement listed here are often known comprehensively as the employee development plan. The focus here is on how the employee can develop his or her skills in order to keep growing in the position, the organization, or the profession. These **development goals** might also be relevant to the employee's own general career plans—beyond the outlines of this particular position or company.

Some development plans are very general, while others are more specific and identify particular actions that the employee agrees to undertake. (In general, the more specific, the better, such as targeting what an employee needs to do over the next two years, rather than "in the future.") Some will include specific time frames; others will just have a general time frame that spans the entire performance measurement period.

Some sample development goals include:

■ Take three two-day training courses or seminars to improve skills or earn degree.

■ Participate in five days of internal training to improve knowledge of spreadsheet applications.

■ Join professional association and attend meetings monthly.

■ Complete refresher course in intermediate Spanish.

This is just a brief list of examples. More details on the employee development plan and development goals can be found in chapter 4.

ASK THE EXPERTS

Should employees' own individual goals get incorporated into the development plan?

Yes. Employees' individual development goals are very important. Ideally, the development section of the appraisal form will provide a way for the employee and the manager to work together on how the employee can further develop skills, areas of knowledge, and behavioral characteristics that will enable the employee to meet and exceed his or her performance goals. In this way, the employee can grow within his or her job, and perhaps even grow within the organization.

FIRST PERSON INSIGHTS
Walking the walk

"In the past, like all the managers at my company, I always left the 'development' section of the appraisal form blank because I didn't really know what it meant. It wasn't until we attended a seminar on doing effective performance appraisals that I learned just how important this section is. Here, an HR expert explained that in order to really plan for our company's future, managers need to brainstorm with employees about how they can improve their skills and professional knowledge, and then we need to support them and provide the resources for them to do that. Sure enough, once we started paying more attention to employee development, we got incredible results: Top employees stopped resigning out of boredom, average employees started achieving much more than before, and underperformers got the training they needed to improve. Company morale and productivity got a big boost, allowing us all to do a better job of planning our company's long-term growth and development. What a great tool!"

Yuen-li C., Bloomfield, IN

The rating system

Most performance appraisal systems require you to assign a rating to each section of the appraisal form, and also to the overall appraisal. Familiarize yourself with your organization's particular rating system now, so you won't be surprised when you have to start thinking in terms of ratings when it's time to fill in the form.

Rating systems vary across organizations. Some rating systems ask you to assign a number from a scale that corresponds to the level of achievement. These systems rely on numbers alone to define levels of performance. Other rating systems ask you to select both a number that corresponds to a level of achievement and a descriptive term (such as "meets standards" or "exceeds expectations").

Some organizations use a five-level rating system, while others use a four-level or three-level system. It's not so important how many levels your form has. What is important is that you understand and can accurately assess what each level means in terms of employee performance.

On many forms, you first need to rate individual goals and competencies, then rate entire sections. There are basically two approaches to rating sections—mathematical and nonmathematical. **Mathematical approaches** provide you with a formula to calculate a rating. Sometimes that formula is weighted, which means that certain goals or competencies are more important than others. Nonweighted formulas require that you calculate a straight average of the applicable goals or competencies.

Nonmathematical approaches don't provide a formula; instead, they ask you to make the best assessment possible based on how the employee performed against the goals that were set at the beginning of the year. If you're evaluating a number of different factors in one section, you will need to use your judgment as to what's most important. If your system is set up like this, be sure that you're consistent in how you apply your judgment from one employee to the next.

RATING SYSTEMS

Here's a look at various rating systems you might encounter while doing performance appraisals:

Nonmathematical

This includes rating systems that use phrases to describe either the performance or the person (this kind of system is not favored these days by management experts, but some companies still use them). These are typical phrases used to describe performance:

Far Exceeds Expectations
Exceeds Expectations
Meets Expectations
Needs Improvement
Unacceptable

Mathematical

These ratings systems use only numbers to evaluate performance and usually consist of a scale of 1 to 5 or 1 to 4. These systems come in two varieties:

■ **Nonweighted** The manager assigns a number that correlates to the employee's performance. All goals and competencies are equally important.

■ **Weighted** Goals and competencies are assigned a weight, or a number that corresponds to how important it is. This number is multiplied by the employee's rating. An example:

Goal	Weight		Employee's rating		Employee's total score
Edit three books	4	X	3	=	12

Other types of appraisals

It may be that your company requires additional types of performance appraisals. Two of these are:

360-Degree or Multirater Appraisals In this type of appraisal, the manager seeks input on the employee's performance from customers, coworkers, direct reports, vendors, and others whom the employee worked with during the performance measurement period. These require careful planning and communication. Often the process is handled by someone outside the organization. Whether handled internally or externally, it's critical that the confidentiality of everyone who participates in a 360-degree appraisal is maintained.

Upward Appraisals In these, employees are asked to evaluate their managers relative to specific expectations and behaviors. Upward appraisals give employees a voice they might not otherwise have— and they give managers information that can help them to improve their effectiveness.

ASK THE EXPERTS

I have never done a 360 review before. How long does it take?

It varies. Some 360 review forms have many open-ended questions that need detailed answers, so this can take a few days. Other forms consist of just a page with boxes to check, so they can be completed in an hour or two. It also depends on the number of people asked to complete an appraisal on the employee. Obviously, the fewer people involved, the faster it will go, although using appraisal software can help speed things up.

I have to do a 360 review and am worried that one particular coworker will say unfavorable things about me. What can I do?

It might help to remember that your boss, if he or she was trained in the process, probably realizes this may happen, and will know to take one person's negative comments in stride if everyone else has good things to say about you. As long as what that person says is not true, you should relax and feel confident that the truth will prevail. If what your coworker will say is true, however, then it's better to explain this to your boss ahead of time so that he or she isn't surprised by the coworker's comments.

I am a pretty hard taskmaster and am concerned that my employees will grumble in my upward appraisal. Will senior management look upon that unfavorably?

That depends. Assuming that senior management knows you are demanding and approves of your style, it should not be an issue. If, however, the issues raised indicate something more serious (for example, if your employees say you are unfair or disrespectful), this will give you some valuable input about changes you need to make. Senior management may indeed not be happy about any serious issues that are raised, but approaching the situation with a willingness to change should help defuse this.

Helpful resources

Tools you can use

BOOKS

Productive Performance Appraisals (The Worksmart Series)
by Randi Toler Sachs

The Performance Appraisal Source Book: A Collection of Practical Examples
by Mike Deblieux

360-Degree Feedback: The Powerful New Model for Employee Assessment and Performance Improvement
by Mark R. Edwards

WEB SITES

Office of Personnel Management
www.opm.gov/perform/overview.asp
The Office of Personnel Management Web site contains lots of information and links to other helpful sources.

Workforce Management
www.workforceonline.com
Contains a wealth of informative articles on performance management.

Business Know-How
www.businessknowhow.com/manage/jobdesc.htm
This links to "How to Write a Job Description," a helpful and thorough article complete with samples.

Yahoo! Groups: Work Performance
http://finance.groups.yahoo.com/group/work-performance
From this link, you can sign up for a moderated and lively discussion that covers topics relating to performance management, appraisals, and improvement.

CHAPTER TWO

GETTING STARTED

Create performance files

One of the best things you can do to ease the performance appraisal process is to start documenting the performance of those who work for you. That means creating a performance file for each employee (some performance appraisal software programs will help you do this quickly and easily). In this file, you should include the employee's job description (see page 14), a copy or his or her goals and development plan from previous performance appraisals, and copies of any written feedback you've been given by other managers about that employee. You may also want to include documents that cover any particular achievements the employee made throughout the year—for example, copies of relevant memos or e-mails. Don't go overboard; this file shouldn't be a duplicate of all of the work the employee has produced during the year; it should just cover the highlights and low spots.

Some managers like to keep a performance log form on each employee. In the log, you'll want to make quick notes about his or her performance throughout the year. It may help you stay more focused if you to write down the specific goal or competency to which the observation or behavior relates. See the sample on page 31.

As you jot things down, remember to keep it simple. Here's how:

■ Describe the employee's behavior as you see it or as you hear it. Leave out any extra interpretations, analysis, or suppositions. In other words, stick to the facts!

■ Be accurate. Don't make any guesses as to what the employee's motivations are. As a manager of performance, you are there to check on performance, not analyze why employees do the things they do.

■ Keep it short. Lengthy stories won't help you speed through appraisals at the end of the year. Maintaining this file consistently should save you time in the long run.

■ Keep it legal. There are basic commonsense rules about fairness and discrimination in the workplace. Ask HR for guidelines.

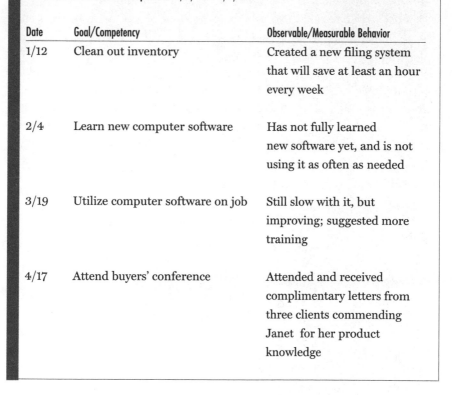

SAMPLE

PERFORMANCE LOG

Employee name: Janet Green
Job title: Assistant Sales Manager
Performance measurement period: 4/1/03–4/1/04

Date	Goal/Competency	Observable/Measurable Behavior
1/12	Clean out inventory	Created a new filing system that will save at least an hour every week
2/4	Learn new computer software	Has not fully learned new software yet, and is not using it as often as needed
3/19	Utilize computer software on job	Still slow with it, but improving; suggested more training
4/17	Attend buyers' conference	Attended and received complimentary letters from three clients commending Janet for her product knowledge

Be fair and accurate

Know what to do to avoid legal pitfalls

The first—and best—rule when it comes to documentation and performance appraisals is to follow the legal guidelines that apply to all aspects of the workplace. Also, you must, in all ways, be fair and accurate. Why is this so important? Because performance appraisals can be used by your employees if they decide to sue your company for some reason (such as alleged discrimination or unfair termination). That's why it's a good idea to talk to your human resources department before you begin. When documenting performance, it's good to keep these principles in mind:

Document accurately and on an ongoing basis. Documentation must be specific, accurate, and focus only on job-related behaviors and actions. Maintain this documentation on an ongoing basis, rather than trying to take notes about the whole performance period right before the performance appraisal meeting or—even worse—right before you take disciplinary action or terminate an employee. In your documentation, take a simple and direct approach. If you document who, what, when, where, why (if you know why), and how, you should have most of the information you need.

Be consistent. Make sure that your system for maintaining employee performance files (see page 30) requires the same kind of documentation for all employees, or you could be accused of targeting a particular group of employees for less favorable treatment because of some shared characteristic. If that shared characteristic happens to be something that is protected by federal, state, or local law, such selective documentation could be perceived as discriminatory.

ASK THE EXPERTS

I asked HR for help in firing a poor performer. They told me I had to go back and document her poor performance first. Why?

You've hit upon one of the most important reasons why managers need to document performance. Without documentation, if you decide to fire this employee, and she decides to challenge it, you may end up with a big legal headache. The best way to avoid this is to maintain documentation (which is just a fancy way of saying "take notes") throughout the year, and to closely follow your organization's disciplinary procedures. This could include verbal warnings, written warnings, or suspension. In your situation, if the employee's performance is bad enough for you to want to fire her, it may not take too long to document her poor performance, and you could be saving yourself a lot of trouble later on. On the positive side, documenting her performance—and giving her feedback about it—might actually help her improve and start meeting expectations, so you might not have to fire her after all!

I have six direct reports and I don't really have the time to do a thorough performance appraisal. Can't I just chat with my employees?

You can, but it won't improve their performance, which is the whole point to the appraisal process! Besides, going through the process will give you valuable insight into how your team functions as well as show your employees that you are involved and supportive of their work.

Even if you do only have informal chats, you need to provide a structure. Such meetings should cover both strong areas and areas that need improvement—and this structure should be the same for all employees.

What documentation does

Besides helping you when it comes time to write performance appraisals, good documentation is a valuable management tool that helps in many other ways:

- Documentation can provide you and your employees with important performance goalposts that you can reference throughout the year.

- Documentation can help you remember much more of what has happened during the performance measurement period. This results in a far more complete representation of each employee's performance—positive and not so positive—during the year.

- Documentation can help smooth the transition for a new manager if you move to another position or organization. It will also help reassure your employees that no matter who their manager is, they will receive consistent and fair performance appraisals that reflect what they've done during the entire performance measurement period, and not just during the tenure of their new manager.

- Documentation can provide important evidence in the event that any of your actions or decisions is challenged, and can help keep situations from escalating. If you ever do end up facing a legal challenge, sound documentation can help you support and defend the decisions you made and the actions you took.

WHAT DOCUMENTATION CAN'T DO

Even a really well-developed documentation system can't do everything. Here are some of the limitations of paperwork:

■ Documentation can't substitute for good management. No amount of detailed documentation of employee behavior can make up for the knowledge and insight you, as a manager, need to bring to the performance appraisal experience.

■ Documentation can't substitute for communication. One of the biggest mistakes managers can make is to use memos in place of face-to-face meetings with employees. Documentation should supplement, not replace, the personal interactions and conversations you need to have with your employees. You can cause irreparable harm to your relationships with your employees if you choose to communicate only in writing about a situation that you should address in person.

■ Documentation can't justify disciplining (or terminating) someone who shouldn't be disciplined or terminated. While documentation can help you defend your actions and decisions if they are called into question, it can do so only if those actions or decisions were appropriate in the first place. No amount of paperwork can turn a poor personnel decision into a good one.

■ Documentation can't substitute for coaching. Even the most motivational and inspiring e-mail can't substitute for one-on-one interaction with your employees.

Documentation anxiety

Tell your employees what you are doing

Sometimes managers hesitate to document the performance of their employees because they worry that their reports will feel spied upon. As a manager, you can work to change your employees' perceptions of written documentation and help make it a more positive experience by following these guidelines:

Tell them what you're doing. Tell your employees that you are going to document performance—before you do it. This way, employees won't wonder what you're doing, or assume that they have done something wrong. Clearly communicate that you are going to document examples of positive performance as well as performance that needs to change.

Tell them why you're doing it. This will help to remove any concerns employees may have that you could have some sort of hidden agenda. Explain to employees how this process will benefit you and them by creating a complete and accurate record of their performance throughout the year. Also let them know that maintaining documentation will help you work with them to address and resolve any performance concerns that might come up—as soon as they come up.

Tell them what you've done. Creating a written record is important—but it's not enough. Documentation needs to be coupled with feedback to be truly effective. That is the whole reason for keeping a file in the first place! If you start seeing a problem emerge from the documents you are collecting, then have a meeting and work out the problem (see chapter 11). Talk with your employee about those aspects of his or her performance that meet expectations, and those that do not.

ASK THE EXPERTS

Should I document every single aspect of performance that I observe, or just note the most significant positive and negative events?

It really depends on what system works best for you. If you usually submit monthly reports on your department's activities, start keeping a monthly—or even weekly—report on your performance observations too. It's easier to adjust an existing process than to create a whole new one. When you're documenting, there is no need to write down what an employee does each day—concentrate on particular achievements or issues, both positive and negative. This is definitely a situation where less is more; use key phrases and words—no need to write a novel. It's fine to just use short phrases that will jog your memory later on, when it's time to do the performance review.

For brand-new managers

Chances are you didn't start out as a manager. Instead, you performed so well in your nonmanagement jobs that you got noticed—and promoted! It can be particularly difficult for those who took this path to get used to evaluating the work of others instead of doing the work themselves. After all, most people like the feeling of doing a good job, which makes it easy for them to fall back into tasks that they know they perform well.

And it can be especially difficult for new managers to suddenly find themselves in a position where they have the responsibility of evaluating—and maybe even disciplining—people who used to be their peers. It's critical in this situation for you to be honest with yourself, and with your direct reports, about how the work relationship has changed. To help set the tone, it's good for managers to have one-on-one meetings with their new direct reports (their old peers) right at the start to discuss in a positive way how things have changed, and how to move forward. Emphasize the ways that you will still be working together and that you will still be approachable, because it's common for old peers to worry that a promotion can "go to your head."

ASK THE EXPERTS

I have two direct reports. In the past I have done both their jobs, so I know all about what is required. I have shown them how to do their jobs, but they keep getting it wrong. I don't want my boss to blame me for their work, so it seems easier to help them to do their job right then document how they are doing it wrong. Am I right?

Not really. Most managers, especially new ones, like to show that they are team players who are always willing to help out. While this may be appropriate sometimes, it's also important to remember that you were promoted because your skills will be even more valuable to your organization if you spend your time coaching others to do a great job too. If your direct reports are not up to the task, then you need to work with them on making their performance better. You may find that it's a good idea to talk to your boss about what's going on, too. You'll still look good (maybe even better) by pointing out problems that need to be fixed.

Managing your feelings

There's no guarantee that you're going to like everyone who works for you. And that's fine—you don't have to. But what you do have to do is to appraise your employees consistently and objectively on the basis of how they perform, regardless of how you happen to feel about them personally.

When it comes to the performance appraisal process, separating the personal from the professional is vital. You don't want your personal feelings to impact how you manage and evaluate your employees. This holds true for those employees you really like, too. When it comes to appraising performance, you need to be able to set your feelings aside.

How do you do this? Here are some general suggestions:

■ Don't deny that you have personal feelings—positive and negative. Accept the way you feel. Don't pretend those feelings don't exist.

■ Make a conscious decision to set aside those feelings at work.

■ Focus on behavior. If you are setting goals, focus on expected behavior. If you are giving feedback, focus on current (or recent) behavior. If you are drafting an appraisal, focus on past behavior. Do your best to keep personal feelings from tainting your assessments.

ASK THE EXPERTS

I have one employee with whom I have some real personality differences. What can I say or do to convince him that my evaluation of his performance is going to be as objective as possible?

The important thing to realize is that you don't have to "convince" your employee that you can be objective when appraisals come around, because you'll be making a point of evaluating him fairly all year long. How? By documenting his performance consistently and regularly, just as you would any other employee's, and by documenting according to the goals you set together at the start of the appraisal period. Then when the performance appraisal meeting happens, if he has any doubt that you are being fair, you will have documentation to support your evaluation. Concentrating on documenting his performance, rather than his personality, should help you steer away from any personal issues you have with him.

One of our employees, Marta, is having problems at home and her work is starting to suffer. I sympathize with her, but should I let this influence how I evaluate her during the performance appraisal?

It's understandable that you would want to cut Marta some slack to avoid giving her a mediocre appraisal, which reflects her actual poor performance. But to obscure the facts and give her a break because of external factors goes against the fundamental idea that performance appraisals are accurate and fair. Plus, giving Marta a "soft" review would not be fair to other employees, who may be working twice as hard or effectively as Marta, and yet might receive a similar review.

The best way to deal with this is to talk with Marta any time you see signs that her performance is slipping—as you would with any employee. That way, she has a chance to do things differently before it's too late. On a personal note, it might even give her something to focus on instead of just her problems at home, and if she can correct her performance, it may give her something to feel good about, too.

How to be objective

Attitude often points to behaviors

A good performance appraisal is objective—meaning it focuses on your employee's behaviors and actions, not his attitude and personality. During the appraisal cycle, then, the goal is to pick up any change in an employee's attitude, but then look past that to see if there are observable behaviors that explain this change. How do you do this? Use your feelings as a starting point—not as an ending point. If you start out thinking about an employee's attitude, just make sure you end up focusing on behavior. For instance, if you find yourself thinking that one of your employees has a really great attitude at work, ask yourself questions that lead to his or her behavior on the job:

■ In what ways is this employee meeting, or exceeding, the expectations of his or her position?

■ In what ways is this person demonstrating the competencies that this organization considers important?

■ In what way is this person acting in accordance with the values of this organization?

■ What is this person doing that reflects well on them, on me, or on the organization?

The same holds true for negative impressions that you might form about an employee's attitude or personality. Again, ask yourself what specific action you are reacting to. It's not enough to say, "It's just a bad feeling I have." Use your reactions as a starting point from which to identify relevant behaviors, then provide feedback about them. For example, if you think that an employee has a poor work attitude, ask yourself if there are any behaviors that result from that attitude, such as coming in late to work, being rude to those who work under him or her, or complaining when new tasks are assigned. That way, you can focus on the behavior, not hard-to-support impressions about attitude.

"Learning to evaluate my employees on the basis of behaviors instead of attitude was a big change for me, and for our company, too. One thing that made it difficult was that 'attitude' was listed for years on our performance appraisal form as a key performance category. But that didn't seem to fit with the emphasis that our new CEO started placing on results when he joined the company three years ago. He kept saying, 'Show your attitude in your work, not just on a motivational poster.' Effort and attitude were still important to him, but by themselves they weren't enough any more. The managers brainstormed on what we thought that really meant, then we took what we came up with and started talking to our employees more about results and behaviors—things that everybody could understand and relate to. Eventually, the appraisal form was updated, and the 'attitude' category was removed. The funny thing is that we really didn't even need that category anymore, since everything we needed to know and observe and evaluate about attitude had been woven into the rest of the form—this time from a results-based perspective, instead of a personality-based perspective."

Lydia S., Naperville, IL

Planning for promotions

One of the purposes of the performance appraisal system, as it pertains to employee development, is to prepare for the future growth of an organization and the employees within it. This requires managers to devote some time to thinking about how the most talented employees, who will likely become even more skilled over time, may at some future date be promoted to more senior positions.

The performance appraisal process, because it supports employees' individual growth, can be particularly helpful for long-term staff planning. When employees strive to develop themselves professionally, it leads to growth within a particular position, and perhaps growth within the organization. It can also help the organization itself grow, which in turn may create more higher-level job openings to which employees may be promoted.

An ideal performance appraisal system should incorporate a developmental component, or development plan (see page 22) to address the need for managers to think long-term about promotions. The development plan enables employees and managers to work together to develop a strategy for the employee's growth and progress up the career ladder.

Working out development plans with employees during the performance appraisal process helps ensure that the right people with the right skills will be ready to move into the right positions at the right time. By plotting future growth, managers determine what the needed skills will be, who should develop those skills, and when and how to go about doing this. Without a performance appraisal system that addresses long-term growth plans, neither the employee nor the organization will be well prepared to meet unexpected requirements in the future.

DON'T AUTOMATICALLY PROMOTE— THINK IT THROUGH

Although there are lots of ways that the performance appraisal process can support employee promotions and succession planning, it's not the answer to everything. Before automatically promoting an employee, it's important to be really familiar with the skills, knowledge, and behavioral characteristics required for a particular position, and to compare them objectively to the candidate's.

The performance appraisal can be helpful in this process, but only to the degree to which the old position and the new one are similar. For example, think about the skills, knowledge, and behavioral characteristics that are required to be an automotive mechanic. Now, think about the skills, knowledge, and behavioral characteristics that might be required of a car repair shop manager. To some degree, the technical ability and expertise that are important for a mechanic to have would still be required for the higher-level position. But there are lots of other skills that would be required as well: customer service skills, conflict resolution skills, and perhaps even budgeting skills. So your best mechanic may not be the best candidate for shop manager. Instead of solving one problem (the job opening) you may create a second: losing your best auto mechanic! So look at each position's requirements independently and realize that performance appraisals are one helpful tool, but not the only tool you need to make promotion and hiring decisions.

Helpful resources

BOOKS

Performance Appraisal: Legal and Effective Management of Performance
by Harvey S. Blustain

The Performance Appraisal Question and Answer Book: A Survival Guide for Managers
by Richard C. Grote and Dick Grote

The Complete Guide to Performance Appraisal
by Richard C. Grote and Dick Grote

WEB SITES

HR Software.Net
www.hr-software.net/
Provides a list of software products where individuals can download demos and trial versions.

HR Software.Net
www.hr-guide.com/data/209.htm
More software products relating specifically to performance appraisal.

Bacall and Associates/ Work911
www.work911.com/performance
Connects to Robert Bacal's consulting service, however it offers a lot of valuable information on performance management—for free.

CHAPTER THREE

ADDRESSING EMPLOYEE CONCERNS

Explain the process

Involving your employees in the appraisal process shows them that you are there not only to help them achieve their goals, but to further their careers. To do that you need to help them develop a clearer understanding of what the appraisal process is all about. But telling your employees about this process one time is not enough. Memos are good, meetings are probably best. (Often, HR departments will conduct informational meetings about performance appraisals for new employees and managers alike.)

Consider holding a meeting with your direct reports at the beginning of the performance measurement period, and another a few months before the end, to let them know what you are doing, and, more importantly, why. In this meeting, you may want to:

- Share the appraisal timeline and the forms.
- Explain the steps you'll be using (mention that you are documenting performance).
- Let them know how important their participation is.
- Outline your responsibilities and their responsibilities.
- Encourage honest communication about what employees are feeling.
- Allow time for discussion, and answer questions candidly.

There may be times, however, when employees don't feel comfortable asking certain questions in public. It's also very likely that employees will think of additional questions after they've had a chance to think about (or talk about) the information you've shared with them. Let employees know that you're available to meet with them individually to answer any questions that might come up. At the beginning, let employees know that you'll also be scheduling individual goal-setting meetings, during which they will have the opportunity to ask questions.

ASK THE EXPERTS

Should I explain the process in a group meeting, or individually to each employee? How much detail do I need to go into?

It depends. Sometimes your organization will make this process a lot easier by giving you a packet of information about performance appraisals, which you can hand out during a group meeting. This might include information sheets and even a Powerpoint presentation.

If your organization doesn't have this packet, it should be easy enough to get this information together. When deciding what to communicate in a group meeting, always ask yourself, "Does this apply to everybody?" Things you might want to discuss in general include: information about the self-appraisal process (see chapter 7), skills that employees will be evaluated on, the appraisal timeline, and, perhaps most importantly, ideas on how employees can get involved in the process. It's also a good idea to allow for a question-and-answer period at the end, but set the rules on this up front. Explain that you're happy to answer general questions about appraisals, but that individual questions are better saved for a one-on-one meeting.

Discuss the impact

Many employees view performance appraisals as a report card that will somehow be used against them. You need to reach out to employees and explain the purpose behind performance appraisals. Here's what you can do to make the appraisal process run smoothly:

Communicate performance expectations in advance. Nervous employees can take comfort in knowing exactly what is expected of them and when. To that end, make sure goals are SMART (see page 68), and that the behaviors on which you are basing your assessments are measurable and/or observable in relation to these goals. Conversely, employees need to know in advance what the consequences of poor performance will be, in terms of retraining, warning, suspension, and so on. These consequences can't come as a surprise. Lay out to your employees not only what you expect them to do, but what will happen if they don't meet those expectations.

Provide open, honest, and ongoing feedback to employees about their performance. Communication is key. Employees need to know how they are performing. Performance appraisals can do wonders to redirect employees who have gotten off track or to remotivate those employees who feel their work is not appreciated.

Encourage employees to ask questions and converse with you. In addition to being a good management practice, performance appraisals sometimes are the best way to open up a dialogue, especially for those employees who find it hard to talk to their managers. Be open to discussing performance challenges and possible solutions; maintain a willingness to support, coach, guide, and direct your employees, while encouraging two-way communication.

"Even though it happened 10 years ago, I can remember that performance review as if it were yesterday. I had been working in sales in a male-dominated high-tech industry. I had to deal with all sorts of characters, but was holding my own. I was doing really well and making a lot in commissions. At the time, I thought performance appraisals were bogus, especially for those of us in sales. When I went for mine, my supervisor told me that I was doing well and had met my objectives. Then she stopped and said: 'The only setback I can see is that you do not speak confidently with senior management. You tend to become very withdrawn. You need to work on that if you want to get ahead.' Me—not confident? Impossible! But after I cooled down and thought about it, I realized she was right. I was intimidated by those guys. I made a concerted effort to change. I initiated contact with senior management whenever I could. I volunteered for jobs where they needed sales support. In due time, I learned to overcome my fears, and senior management noticed. I was promoted and given the best sales territory in the entire company. That performance appraisal turned my career around. I sometimes tell this story to my reports to let them know just how important an appraisal can be to them."

Eve P., Bedford, NY

Compensation concerns

Don't let money become the main focus of the appraisal process

Many employees (and managers) link the performance appraisal system to salary review or promotion. These employees think their performance appraisal should validate their desire for a raise or promotion. But the truth is, the issue of compensation or promotion is usually better addressed separately from the appraisal process. Why? There are a lot of reasons. For starters, a company may be in a flat or down cycle and unable to give any raises. Or the company may have laid off a portion of its employees and therefore no promotions may be in the wings. The point you need to stress is that performance appraisal is about just that: their performance as it compares to their stated goals and objectives. Talk about money and promotions separately. Here are some common employee mindsets you may encounter:

"If my pay isn't tied to how well I perform, what difference does it make how I perform in my job?" In some organizations, pay increases aren't connected in any way to performance. If that's the case where you work, this is what you might hear. If you do, take this as a sign that you have an opportunity to find out how to motivate such employees to perform better. You need to learn what makes them tick and figure out how to motivate them. You can try recognition or additional responsibilities. You can also try to help these employees find ways to motivate themselves.

"My rating is determined by how much money they can afford to give out this fiscal year, not by how well I performed." This can be a very powerful belief on the part of your employees—one that can really serve to negatively impact employee performance. You need to explain that employees' performance ratings are based on how well they meet their goals and objectives. Whether your company is in the position to give out raises or not is moot.

"This appraisal can't mean anything—because I know I'm worth more than a 3% raise." Be careful that employees do not define their job performance by the percentage increase they receive. Even in pay-for-performance systems, the dollar amount increase or the percentage increase is determined by a number of different factors—not just by how well the employee performed or by the employee's overall rating.

"I exceeded expectations this year—but I'm not getting an increase. The guy I work next to just told me that he was rated as 'meets expectations,' and he got a 2% increase. There's no way this performance management system can be fair." Have no doubt—your employees will compare information about their performance ratings and about their merit increase amounts. To prevent misunderstandings from arising, make sure each of your employees understands how the system works, and that they can't make meaningful comparisons between one person's raise and another's. For instance, employees—especially outstanding employees—may "max out" their salary range and be ineligible for a pay increase. (They may only get an increase if they are promoted and enter a higher salary range.)

New staff members

New members of your team, be they newly hired, transferred, or promoted employees, are often worried that they will not be evaluated fairly if your company's performance appraisals are done at a set time each year and they have only been on the job a short time before that date. What should you do?

Whenever a new team member comes aboard, you should have a meeting and go over goals and objectives. Tell these new reports when performance appraisals are due and how you intend to handle them, given their short time on the job. Most companies have managers do a performance appraisal regardless of when the employee started, as a way of providing formal feedback. Even employees who may not be eligible for a merit increase, or who will receive a prorated increase, should participate in the appraisal process.

Newly hired employees
The most important thing to keep in mind with newly hired employees is that you've got to sit down with them and develop collaborative goals as soon as they come on board. Channel the excitement and nervous energy that new employees bring with them into developing and attaining goals and objectives for the performance measurement period. Realize that there's going to be a learning curve for any new employee in any new job, but don't allow that to change your expectations for the position; just keep in mind that it may take the new employee some time to fulfill those expectations. Also, remember that newly hired employees are not only learning their new jobs, they're also learning the culture of their new organization. Be patient, be there to support them, and provide lots of feedback.

Transferred or promoted employees

Employees who transfer from another position or department within your organization already know the culture of your organization, but they still need time to learn their job and to learn the "subculture" of their new department. Just as with your new employees, don't miss the opportunity to develop goals collaboratively with newly transferred employees as soon as they come on board. Sometimes managers assume that an employee who transfers or was promoted from another department will automatically have a good feel for what the goals in the new position should be, since they are already working for the organization and are supporting the same general mission. This doesn't happen automatically, though, and you need to set new goals with a transferred employee, just as you would with a newly hired one. When it comes time for a performance appraisal, you will need to get input from his or her previous manager. Hopefully, that manager has maintained good documentation on the employee's performance.

Employees in new positions

It's particularly important to pay close attention to these employees, whether they have been newly hired, transferred, or promoted. In addition to the uncertainty common with other hiring situations, newly created positions are, by definition, still in the process of being defined. Sometimes job descriptions are very broad. Or performance goals for the position may not exist. Try to set aside time throughout the year to meet with such employees to review and update goals and objectives and to make sure the job description is still accurate and complete. If not, update it—either on your own or with someone from HR—as you go along.

Involve your employees

Work with your employees during the performance appraisal process

There are some managers who believe they can control every aspect of an employee's performance. However, the truth is that you cannot really force employees to perform exactly as you want. To a large degree, employees choose how they are going to perform and the level of achievement they are going to aim for.

The key question, then, becomes how you as the manager can positively influence your employees so that they will choose to perform well. One of the best things you can do to encourage your employees to meet or exceed expectations (both theirs and yours) is to actively involve them in the performance appraisal process by seeking their input, ideas, and feedback about how the system should work. This will help them develop a sense of ownership and responsibility for their performance. And when the responsibility is in their hands, you'll be much more likely to see them pushing themselves harder than even you would—and great results will naturally follow.

Your goal is to get your employees to view the performance appraisal not as something that "happens" to them, but as something in which they have a stake—and a voice. Things that just "happen" to people are (or at least feel) out of their control. In contrast, your employees need to recognize that they have choices in terms of how they perform, and that these choices will have a direct impact on the feedback they receive from you and on their year-end appraisal. Employees who feel that feedback sessions or appraisal meetings are events over which they have little control will be less likely to choose to perform at or above the standards set, so learn to involve them in every part of the appraisal system. They also need to know that they have you to assist and support them in this process.

WHAT IT MEANS TO BE A
GOOD MANAGER OF PERFORMANCE

Being a good manager of your employees' performance means providing timely and focused feedback, as well as involving your employees in the performance appraisal process by doing the following:

- Pointing things out—especially things the employee might not see.
- Being honest—even when it's difficult.
- Giving the employee the benefit of the doubt, and listening to the employee's viewpoint.
- Knowing what your responsibilities are, and following through on them.

Involving your employees in the appraisal process shows that you trust them, which will inspire them to perform well. So set goals with them (see chapter 4), discuss specifics about their performance with them (see chapter 12), and ask them to appraise their own performance at the end of the performance measurement period (see chapter 6). This approach can yield more positive, productive, and lasting results than what you would achieve by trying to "make" employees perform well.

Helpful resources

Tools you can use

BOOKS

The Thin Book of 360 Feedback: A Manager's Guide
by Michelle Leduff Collins

Performance Appraisal: Legal and Effective Management of Performance
by Harvey S. Blustain

Performance Appraisal: Legal Aspects (Technical Report Series #3)
by J. Vernon Odom
and J. Keith Edwards

WEB SITES

Society for Human Resource Management
www.shrm.com
The Society for Human Resource Management (SHRM) Web site contains much valuable information on performance appraisal. Access to much of this site, however, is limited to members.

CharityVillage.com
www.charityvillage.com/CV/ research/rhr8.html
A helpful article on "Painless Performance Appraisals," by Teresa Howe, CHRP.

ULiveandLearn
www.uliveandlearn.com/lessons/ lesson.cfm?lesid=267&pg=1
"Ten tips for Effective Performance Appraisals," by The Writing Center, Inc.

SETTING GOALS

The art of goal setting

The performance goals you and your employees set will play a major role in shaping their careers as well as yours! If the goals you set are uninspiring, such as "complete all assignments on time," or they are off target, for example, "sell 10% more widgets," when your company is pushing to sell its services, not its products, then neither you nor your employees will succeed. But if you set specific, on-target, challenging, measurable goals, then you are helping your employees grow as well as ensuring your success as their manager.

How do you go about setting these all-important goals? Ideally, you should have a meeting just before the start of the new performance appraisal period to determine employees' performance goals. This meeting should last a half hour to an hour. Have a copy of the organization's goals and your department's goals to refer to as you go through the process. Listen carefully as each employee tells you his or her specific goals. Don't confuse goals with tasks. Goals should represent an end result, not an ongoing activity. For example, "ensuring good working relations with employees" is an ongoing activity; but "increasing productivity by 10%" is a goal.

During this meeting, the employee should work out roughly four to six major goals. Encourage the employee to determine the specifics of each goal if you can. (See pages 68–69 on how to refine those goals.) Provide feedback relative to your goals, the goals of the position, and the organization's goals to make sure the employee's goals are in sync. Also, ask the employee to work out the details about how these goals will be accomplished. After you have finalized this part, have the employee send you an e-mail listing the goals, and put a copy of this in the employee's performance file. Then, throughout the year, track the employee's progress toward meeting these goals, keeping notes in the performance file (see page 30). Use these notes to help you write the performance appraisal at the end of the appraisal period.

TASKS VS. GOALS

To help you and your direct reports get the ball rolling and avoid confusing activities and goals during the goal-setting process, keep these basic questions in mind:

- What is the major function of your direct report's job?
- What are the outputs of the position?
- How would this department, or this organization, be impacted if this position didn't exist?

Here are some specific examples of "tasks or activities" vs. "goals or outcomes":

- For the manager of a bowling alley, oiling the lanes and cleaning the pin-setting machines are activities—ensuring that all lanes remain operational at least 98% of the time is a goal.
- For a recruiter, interviewing is an activity—making a hiring recommendation or selection is a goal.
- For a manager, delivering performance appraisals is an activity—ensuring that employees meet or exceed individual goals through an ongoing process of performance management is a goal.

Your organization's goals

Know what senior management wants

Before you can set goals with employees, you need to know your company's overall goals. Why? Because there is no point in setting goals that run counter to the goals senior management is seeking. Companies these days need to be able to respond quickly to changes in the marketplace and use performance goals to do that. For example, in the 80s when IBM was losing market share in the highly competitive PC computer industry, senior management decided to downsize the business of manufacturing PCs and get into the PC-consulting business, providing integrated business solutions. That kind of turnaround called for setting new goals. Those goals started with senior management and worked their way down into the field. In other words, goals cascade from the top down; and as they cascade down, they become more and more individualized. Then, as these individual goals are attained, they build into an upward spiral of success. In short, every employee's goals should be aligned with and support the highest goals of your organization. In IBM's case, they succeeded in changing their corporate strategy by setting new goals.

This top-down approach has an added benefit: It will help each and every employee understand exactly how his or her job contributes to attaining the organization's overall goals. This can create a feeling of belonging and a greater sense of shared effort. It also ensures that everybody's effort and work matters, and minimizes overlap and wasted time and effort.

NOTE: Goals need to be revisited throughout the performance appraisal period, and may need to be modified. This is a sign of your organization's flexibility and adaptability—not its weakness.

ASK THE EXPERTS

There is a lot of talk in my company about responding more quickly to the marketplace, but no real guidelines on how to do that. Do I need to find out what senior management is seeking before I set goals with my direct reports?

Yes. Always make sure you have your company's goals, your boss's goals, and your own goals in writing before having goal-setting meetings with any of your employees. That's the best way—and one of the only ways—to make sure your direct reports' goals relate directly to what really matters most to your organization.

In this case, to find out what is meant by "responding more quickly to the marketplace," try to set up brief meetings with your boss and/or senior management and get more specifics. Ask your boss what he or she really needs and values from you—as opposed to what you've always produced in the past. Also ask how your boss's work is evaluated and how you can help him or her succeed.

You can use the same process you use with your employees to get down to specifics with senior management: Ask what their goals are, how success will be measured, what the time frame for completion is, what process or techniques should be used, and who will be responsible. You can also learn more about your organization's objectives by reading press releases, attending meetings outside of your department if possible, and staying current with the news on your company's Web site.

Your own goals

The best way to ensure your success

Through the goal-setting process, you need to ensure that your employees' performance goals reflect and support your own performance goals. More and more managers are being asked to take on additional responsibilities besides just managing. As a manager, it's important for you to delegate some of that work. You can't—and shouldn't—do it all yourself. So creating goals that are linked to your employees' will give them a chance to develop their talents and to participate more actively in the management of their own performance. You'll become more effective, and you'll work smarter rather than harder. And your employees will appreciate the opportunities you've given them to build their skills.

This also works with your own manager. Use the top-down/bottom-up goal-setting process to learn more about your manager's responsibilities. Explore ways to align your work objectives more closely with those of your manager. Discuss the possibility of taking on additional responsibilities, if that's appropriate. Demonstrate your value, build on it, and focus your efforts on what really matters most—both to you and to your manager.

ASK THE EXPERTS

I was promoted to department manager right after the start of the perform-ance appraisal period. Do I need to set new goals with my direct reports, or can I just rely on the ones that were set before I got here?

It depends on the goals that were set. One of the first things you need to do is meet with employees to discuss their goals and get an update on their progress toward reaching them. Then you need to determine if those goals are in keeping with your goals (see page 64) and the company's goals (see page 62). If the former goals need to be altered, have a meeting with each employee and formally change them.

I don't have time to meet with all my direct reports about their goals. Can I do it via e-mail?

E-mail is a great way of communicating about many things in the workplace. It can be an especially useful tool for helping you manage your employees and share information. It's not, however, an appropri-ate substitute for a face-to-face goal-setting meeting. The time you invest in this meeting will have a huge impact on how employees per-form throughout the year. Nothing can substitute for this face-to-face encounter, where reactions and responses will be spontaneous, not scripted as they may be in an e-mail. In this way, meetings can shed much light on employees' true thoughts and motivations. But while you do not want to engage in the goal-setting process via e-mail, it can be used to share drafts of goals and to document how you have arrived at their final versions.

Employees' goals

Define goals by position, not by individual potential

How should goals be set for employees who have the same job title, but who have demonstrated different levels of performance, ability, or potential? This is every manager's concern. Generally speaking, employees who hold the same job title and perform the same functions should have similar goals. Setting different goals for people who do the same exact job can demotivate employees if they feel they're being evaluated differently from other employees. This is especially true if they feel that more is expected of them than of coworkers in the same position.

This doesn't mean, however, that all employees who hold the same job title should have identical goals. After all, not every job can be measured by how much of a particular product is produced or how much profit is earned. Sometimes employees who have the same job title support the department and the manager in different ways, using different skills, or have been in the same job for different lengths of time. In this case, goals may differ somewhat from employee to employee. But even if the responsibilities of employees in this position aren't exactly the same, the overall amount of work expected and difficulty of their goals need to be comparable.

Goal-setting should always be a collaborative process. And remember that goals are not nearly as effective when they are assigned to employees as they are when employees participate in developing them.

WHAT IF?

What if I haven't completed my own goals by the time my employees need to begin drafting their goals?

Sit down with your employees and share with them as much information about your goals as you can. Make the conversation as interactive as possible. Encourage them to ask lots of questions. This will give your employees the best possible starting point for drafting their goals. Then give your direct reports your actual written goals as soon as possible. If necessary, work with your employees to revise their goals if your final goals end up changing significantly (although, generally speaking, goals tend not to change drastically from year to year). Although this is not an ideal situation, remember that it's better to provide your employees with interim goals to work toward rather than not providing them with any goals at all.

What if no other managers in my organization discuss their goals with their employees? Can I still use this approach?

Yes. The top-down/bottom-up approach to goal-setting can work just as well for one manager as it does for a whole organization. Your employees will appreciate your efforts, and you'll have a great management tool. Consider visible ways of motivating your workers, such as posting goals in the shape of a pyramid on a bulletin board in your work area. Once other managers see how well this technique works, you may not be the only manager using this approach for long.

The SMART approach

Groom your employees for success right from the start

Setting goals with your employees doesn't have to be daunting if you use the **SMART** approach. The first formulation of SMART guidelines was developed in the 1960s by the management guru Peter Drucker to help managers set specific, objective, measurable goals. This way managers can focus on an employee's behavior, and not get caught up in personality issues—be they positive or negative.

In the latest iteration of this approach, here is what SMART goals stand for:

Specific: In describing the goal, use words that are clear and unambiguous, and thus not open to different interpretations by different people. (For more on this, see page 70.)

Measurable: Set measurable goals so that you—and your employees—will know when you have reached them (see page 72 for more). Usually, this means setting a quantity or quality goal, such as a number of items to produce, or a goal for the quality of those items.

Action-Oriented: The first word in every goal should be a robust verb that powerfully describes the results that will be attained. For example, you might use the words "implement" or "launch" when talking about the roll-out of a new software system. (For more on this, see page 74.)

Realistic: Goals must be realistic and attainable (though this may mean different things to different managers). Here is an example: "Increase production of baseball bats by 10% within six months." (For more on this, see page 76.)

Time-bound: Specify a date by which a goal must be met, such as in two months' time or by the next quarter. (For more on this, see page 78.)

"Writing SMART goals was a totally different approach for me. At first I was worried that if I set really specific goals, my employees would think that I did not take into consideration how hard they tried. I manage a graphic design studio, so effort makes a big difference. What ended up happening, though, was completely different from what I feared. I got my employees involved in the process right from the start and helped them set realistic goals for themselves. They were glad to be involved, but it really made the biggest difference with Murphy, a designer who seemed to spend almost as much time complaining about work as he did designing. Six months into this new process, Murphy realized that setting SMART goals didn't mean I was going to become rigid or inflexible. Murphy and I met throughout the year to review his design goals and make sure they were still realistic. When they weren't, we adjusted them—and Murphy was sold on the process! Overall, using SMART goals has helped me become a better manager—and has helped my employees (especially Murphy) feel better about working for me."

Grant L., Beverly, MA

"S" is for specific

Keep employees from "guesstimating" about goals

Goals aren't intended to be a list of all of the duties that an employee is supposed to perform. If that were the case, each employee would have hundreds—or even thousands—of goals. Instead, it might be helpful to think of goals as "buckets," or "umbrellas." This means each goal has lots of tasks associated with it, and these tasks come beneath the general umbrella, or fall within the overall bucket, that is defined by the goal. For example, a goal that involves hiring five employees within three months would involve a variety of tasks, including writing an ad and placing it, screening résumés, interviewing candidates, and checking references.

To work, goals must be specific in order to minimize the likelihood that employees will misdirect and waste their efforts. If employees don't have specific criteria about their goals, a lot can be left to chance. Some employees may try on their own to define what you mean by a goal you set but don't specify. These "guesstimates" may or may not align with your departmental goals and with what you actually need the employee to accomplish. Worse, some employees will just go through the motions of their job and assume all is well instead of working toward specific outcomes, because none were stated.

So what's the best way to make goals specific? Developing specific goals has to do with identifying specific outcomes, not with listing every task that needs to be accomplished in order to attain those outcomes. Think of the four to six outcomes you want this employee to accomplish. Brainstorm with your employee for ideas and write down those goals. Use words that hone the goal even more; for example, instead of writing "increase productivity," use "increase productivity in Latin American markets by 10%." Next, write down those tasks that will help make that goal happen, such as "improve quality by 10%, cut wholesale costs by 5%, and hire three more on-site reps."

ASK THE EXPERTS

Won't my employees feel a little insulted if I focus on specifics, and think I'm implying that they don't know what they are supposed to be doing in their own jobs?

Sure, if you dictate goals to your employees without asking for their input, they could possibly feel insulted. Your direct reports could also react negatively if goals become a detailed laundry list of everything they are supposed to be doing. If you use this process, however, as an opportunity to share ideas about organizational objectives and to discuss how each employee can support and contribute to achieving those objectives, goal setting can become a springboard to better understanding and a better relationship.

I have one employee who is resisting setting specific goals, preferring to keep them general. She believes her main strength is her flexibility and that specific goals will limit her productivity. How can I convince her otherwise?

It's crucial for you to help her understand that setting vague goals does not improve flexibility, but rather can lead to confusion, false starts, and wasted effort. Even if she has a particularly wide-ranging job description, with lots of general tasks, that does not mean her goals need to be similarly general. When it comes down to it, both you and the employee need to know specifically what she is supposed to accomplish if you are to be able to evaluate her performance and reward her accordingly. Remind her that not all goals have to be measurable in numbers, which may seem limiting; some goals can be more about the quality of performance, the environment for success that the employee creates around her, and the fruitfulness of her interactions with coworkers or clients.

"M" is for measurable

A goal is only useful if you can measure its success

Yogi Berra once said, "You got to be very careful if you don't know where you're going, because you might not get there." In the same way, goals need to be measurable for managers to know where they're going and to figure out whether or not they have arrived!

Measurements, or measures, are standards that are incorporated into goals to let employees know exactly what they are expected to accomplish. They also give managers and employees a common reference point against which to compare each employee's performance during the performance measurement period. These same measures will be used at the end of the performance measurement period to evaluate and assess the degree to which employees met their goals.

There are many ways to build measures into performance goals. Different types of measures are more appropriate in different organizations and in different situations. Keep in mind that you need to build in **quantity measures** (how much is attained), as well as **quality measures** (how well the achievements meet quality standards).

Here are some standard quantitative measures:

Volume How much of a certain item must be produced? For instance, a volume goal might be to produce 30,000 bars of soap. Or, it might be to develop three new varieties of soap.

End Dates By what date does the employee need to attain these goals? Do you expect your employees to sell 30,000 widgets per day, per week, per month, or per year? Or, by what date do you expect your employees to develop those new varieties? End dates help ensure that goals remain time-bound. (This is the "T" in SMART. See page 78.)

Cycle Time How long does it take to complete a specific (and usually recurring) task from start to finish? Shorter cycle times can result in higher volume and/or reduced costs. For instance, how long does it take to produce one can of soup? Or, how long does it take to develop and introduce a new variety of soup?

Unit Cost What does it cost to produce one unit, or to complete one cycle? Reducing unit costs improves efficiency and saves money. For instance, what does it cost to manufacture one T-shirt? Or, what does it cost to develop and introduce a new style of T-shirt?

Here are some standard qualitative measures:

Success Rate This refers to the degree to which specific measures of quality are attained. How well something is completed is just as important—and sometimes even more important—than how much of something is completed. Success rate shouldn't always be set at 100%; although this might be admirable, it may not be realistic. For instance, in a soap factory, it might be commendable to hope that 100% of ingredients purchased will be used to manufacture sellable soap. The reality, however, is that things can and do go wrong: Ingredients can expire, additives or dyes can be spilled, packages can be crushed. In this case, a challenging utilization rate for ingredients might be 92%, 95%, or 98%. Work with your employees and managers to identify challenging and realistic success rates.

Utilization Rate This refers to the percentage of use of a product or service. If, for example, 90 out of 100 customers at your shop pay for gift-wrapping, the utilization rate for this service is 90%. The ideal utilization rate for your company's and employees' goals is determined largely by your service or product, and so it can run anywhere from 5 to 100%.

"A" is for action-oriented

Jump-start your goals with active verbs

Making goals action-oriented brings them to life. This means using active, powerful verbs to describe them. Doing this not only makes goals more vibrant, it help ensure that they are based on actual outcomes, not just on tasks or activities, because strong action verbs are always more specific and clearer than more general ones. Action oriented goals should start with strong action verbs. This approach may already be familiar to you if you used it when writing your résumé (the first word next to each bullet in a résumé should always be a strong action verb). Good action-oriented verbs include *delivered*, *achieved*, *generated*, and *streamlined*.

Match these verbs with specific goals. For example, take a look at how strong verbs are paired with outcomes in the action-oriented goals that follow:

Sales Generate monthly revenue of $80,000 with a median per-sale amount of at least $15,000.

Manufacturing Write, edit, print, and distribute two 50-page books on popular card games by the end of the fiscal year.

Service Resolve 80% of incoming customer service phone calls to the customer's satisfaction within three minutes.

As you work to develop action-oriented goals, talk with employees, colleagues—and check out a thesaurus! And remember: The idea isn't to use more or bigger words. The idea is to use better, clearer, more action-oriented ones.

For a list of useful active verbs that may give you some ideas, see page 121.

ACTION-ORIENTED GOALS

Suppose that you are the manager of a public relations agency. You have six employees—three are associates and three are support staff. Consider the difference that setting action-oriented goals can make:

Example 1

Task-oriented goal: Produce new-client project proposals quickly.

Action-oriented goal: Produce new-client project proposals within three business days of set-up meeting.

Example 2

Task-oriented goal: Respond to calls and e-mails promptly and professionally.

Action-oriented goal: Respond to calls within same business day and to e-mails within 24 hours. Always address callers by name. Use company e-mail templates and proper salutations in e-mails.

Obviously, the action-oriented goals are more precise, with defined targets. This helps make the goals more concrete, which will help employees feel that they are achievable.

"R" is for realistic

Rome was not built in a day

Very often, children—and even adults—are told to set their goals higher than they think they can ever attain. Usually people who suggest this shoot-for-the-moon approach believe that, while you may not achieve your goal, you will accomplish more than you would have if the goal had been set lower. For this reason, some managers set unrealistically high goals because they think that setting attainable goals will stop their employees from trying to improve. These manager truly believe that they are inspiring their employees to keep trying harder.

That may be true sometimes. However, there is often a price to pay for this approach. While employees may indeed accomplish more, they may still feel they failed to reach their goals. And as long as this approach to goal setting is used, employees will continue to fail over and over again, creating a cycle of failure. And employees are not likely to stay in a situation in which they believe that they will always fail. Instead, work to develop collaborative goals with your employees that are reasonable, attainable, and linked to the organization's goals.

ASK THE EXPERTS

Setting realistic goals for employees is extremely hard for me—I'm always tempted to expect more. How do I know what is realistic?

One way to bring your expectations back into line with reality is to ensure that employees' individual goals are relevant to the "bigger picture." This means making sure that individual goals are linked to your organization's overall goals (see page 62). Using the top-down/bottom-up approach to goal setting will ensure that this linking takes place. Also, try to set goals that are appropriate in the culture of your organization. For example, does the culture of your company include the expectation of a 40-hour workweek? An 80-hour one? Is collaboration valued over individual contributions, or is the opposite true? Are creativity and innovation paramount, or are employees expected to follow established patterns? Staying attuned to the wider context by asking yourself these kinds of questions will go a long way toward keeping employees' goals relevant and your expectations realistic.

Two of my employees claim that their individual goals are impossible to reach due to a lack of company resources. How can I lower frustration levels and set more realistic goals?

Setting realistic goals requires you to recognize and respect organizational and economic realities so that you don't end up expecting the impossible. This means making sure that employees will have the resources they need to reach their goals—before you set them. Depending upon the specific goal, these resources, or tools, could include money, time, head count, or organizational support and buy-in. If your employees have all the tools they need at their disposal, they'll be much less likely to feel frustrated by goals that they feel are unrealistic. If you can't provide the necessary resources, then you need to change the goals.

"T" is for time-bound

Because late is sometimes worse than never

Keeping goals to a set time means establishing clear expectations relative to the dates by which employees need to attain specific goals. Without end dates, goals lack specificity; moreover, employees lack the ability to learn how to schedule and manage their time effectively, and managers lose out on a valuable way to supervise a project.

Knowing the time frame within which goals must be attained also adds accountability to the whole process. Your employees want to know what is expected of them and when it is expected. Most employees also like to have some degree of control over their work and their goals. Setting time parameters for completion supports these self-management principles and increases employees' accountability to their managers—and to themselves.

Specifying end dates also helps to avoid some of the problems that can arise when employees or managers make assumptions. For instance, if no end date is specified, employees may assume that the manager does not really expect the goal to be delivered until the end of the performance measurement period. They may think that the manager just wants them to "do their best" and make "as much progress as possible." The manager, conversely, may make the assumption that the employee knows that the goal must be completed as soon as possible, so that other goals can be set in place.

Specifying end dates creates much more clarity and specificity than just asking employees to "do their best," and avoids the problems that can arise from unspoken assumptions. So think hard about a reasonable time frame for each goal (based on the expectations for the position, not the person). Then specify time frames and an end date—and put them in writing.

CAST GOALS IN CLAY, NOT CONCRETE

It can be really tempting to hold on tightly to a particular goal throughout the entire performance measurement period, no matter what happens! After all, you and your employees worked hard to develop these goals and deliver them at the set time. However, a goal that makes sense at the beginning of the year may not make any sense at all three months later. Or, what is realistic in June may be completely different from what was realistic in January. They may be SMART goals, but they must also be the correct goals. Be willing to revisit goals on a quarterly basis to ensure that what started out SMART still is. Encourage your employees to do the same. Use regular feedback discussions as an opportunity to formalize this process. Be flexible. Your employees will appreciate you for it, and the organization will value you for your responsiveness and adaptability.

Securing employee buy-in

Personal commitment can make all the difference

No performance appraisal system will ever truly succeed unless employees' involvement evolves into personal commitment, otherwise known as employee buy-in. Since goal setting takes place at the beginning of the performance appraisal process, it represents your first—and best—opportunity to strengthen employees' commitment to the overall process, and to their own individual goals.

The top-down/bottom-up approach to goal setting provides an ideal backdrop for encouraging involvement that will lead to buy-in. As the manager, you play a key role in cultivating this involvement. Here are some practical ways to stimulate this:

Encourage open discussion. When you share your own goals with employees, invite them to ask questions—even challenging ones—about the goals you have established with your manager, how those goals relate to the company's goals, and how they impact other employees.

Have employees prepare the first draft of their own goals. You are not doing your employees any favors by drafting their goals for them. The activity of translating your goals into their goals will reinforce the relevance of your goals in their minds, plus allow them to play an active role in the creation of their own set of realistic goals.

Discuss the proposed goals with your employees. Ask lots of questions and listen carefully to the answers. In fact, try to do more listening than talking, and use this exchange as an opportunity to learn more about how your employees view their roles. Then use this discussion and the information you collect to enhance your relationship with each of your direct reports.

Don't assume that employees have already bought in to this process. Silence does not necessarily mean agreement. Pay attention to nonverbal communication cues (see page 164).

Developing goals that are SMART may seem challenging at first. But after some practice, you and your employees will find that making goals SMART becomes almost second nature. Without realizing it, you will start to automatically ask yourself whether a particular goal is phrased specifically, or if it is truly measurable. Better yet, so will your employees!

Once you have developed this level of comfort with SMART goals, the next step is to make sure you can be flexible about the goals that you and your employees have developed.

Helpful resources

Tools you can use

BOOKS

The Manager's Guide to
Performance Reviews
by Robert Bacal

Goal Setting (Worksmart Series)
by Susan B. Wilson

Motivation and Goal Setting: How
to Set and Achieve Goals and
Inspire Others
by Jim Cairo

WEB SITES

eCornell
www.eCornell.com/catalog/hr
/ilrhr512.jsp
Cornell University offers an online workshop entitled "Achieving Year-Round
Performance Management and Appraisal,"
which includes a section on goal-setting.

The Management Assistance
Program for Nonprofits
www.mapnp.org/library/emp_perf
/emp_perf.htm
Contains links to information on goal setting and other aspects of performance
management.

Zigon Performance Group
www.zigonperf.com
Sponsored by the Zigon Performance
Group, this site contains a wealth of man-
agement-related information.

CHAPTER FIVE

THE DEVELOPMENT PLAN

The value of development goals

Why they go beyond performance goals

Unlike performance goals, development goals do not necessarily relate to quality or quantity, but rather to tasks or training that an employee can complete to gain deeper expertise or add new skills. They usually are about further training employees so that they are better able to take on new tasks. Development goals do not always have to align directly with organizational objectives, and some may have more to do with an employee's professional objectives. For example, if you have an employee on your team who is very interested in the latest marketing software, a development goal might be to let him or her take classes in the software so he or she can act as your team's facilitator with your company's tech department. While development of this sort benefits the organization, it can also help individuals meet their long-term career objectives.

To determine these goals, you need to ask each employee to think about these questions:

- What does the employee ultimately want to do or to be professionally?
- What are his or her long-term goals?
- What does the employee need to do in the next one to three years in order to reach these goals?

You might want to send these goals in an e-mail before you sit down and officially work them out.

DEVELOP EMPLOYEES:
GIVE THEM WAYS TO GROW

Here are just a few ideas for development opportunities you can give to your employees:

Education Many organizations offer partial or full tuition reimbursement for employees who wish to pursue educational opportunities. The result? You'll have better-educated employees who put their knowledge to work for you.

Training Many organizations offer employees the opportunity to enroll in noncredit workshops, seminars, and certificate programs on specific topics. These training opportunities can provide participants with hands-on skills and knowledge that can be applied in the workplace.

On-site Training Development can take place at the workplace, too! Many companies have on-site training programs. See page 93 for a list.

Temporary Assignments If it's workable—and appropriate—consider placing employees on temporary assignments in areas within the organization where they can develop new skills and expand their knowledge. Temporary assignments may also solve staffing issues caused by short-term leaves of absence, vacationing employees, newly emerging business needs, and peak busy periods.

Special Projects If a temporary assignment isn't feasible, it may be possible to find a special project that an employee can work on that will help him or her learn new skills.

Development goal meetings

Ideally, you want to meet with your each of your employees before the performance appraisal period starts to work out three to five short- or long-term development goals for the year. This meeting is not nearly as formal or structured as the meeting you need to have for setting performance goals (see chapter 4). You can meet with each employee in your office and talk about his or her development needs. Take notes, but be sure to ask your employees to send you an e-mail with their development goals after your meeting. As you work out the specifics of each development goal, be sure to stick to the following guidelines when talking them out:

■ **Keep it SMART** Like performance goals, development goals should be specific, measurable, action-oriented, realistic, and time-bound.

■ **Keep it job-related** Development goals, like performance goals, should relate to the employee's job, chosen field/profession, and the goals of the organization. And like performance goals, they will vary by employee.

■ **Keep up with progress during the year** Get regular updates from employees about how they are progressing toward their development goals. Just as with performance goals, you don't want to find out at end of the year that they have been struggling to meet these goals, and have given up.

ASK THE EXPERTS

I am confused. What is the difference between a development goal and a performance goal?

The difference boils down to this: development goals are about enhancing the quality of an employee's job skills and knowledge, while performance goals are about setting the right benchmarks for their job performance. Here's an example: Imagine you have an employee who has not been very accurate in the last year with some minor accounting calculations. A performance goal for him in the coming year might be to reduce the error rate in his reports to 2%, while a related development goal might be for the employee to attend an accounting refresher course, and perhaps an advanced class later on. Both development and performance goals need to reflect the latest strategic goals of the company.

How long should a development goal meeting take?

If you have both done your homework—you have thought about the training courses your company could offer this individual and the employee has thought about his or her goals—then the meeting should take no more than 30 minutes.

Get employees on board

As you work with employees to set development goals, you may find some who are not eager to take on these growth opportunities. There are a number of different reasons why this may happen.

Time constraints There are just so many hours in the day. Taking time out of a busy day to develop new skills can be the straw that breaks the camel's back. This is especially true for those employees who are working at top speed and have no downtime in their day. It is also an issue for those employees who have personal priorities outside of work—such as family needs or a creative project. The bottom line is that as long as your employees are meeting the performance goals of their positions, it really is their choice whether or not they want to concentrate right now on branching out and developing new skills. While being respectful of employees' personal priorities, however, you do need to make sure they are prepared for how their jobs will change in the near future and ensure that they will maintain an appropriate level of knowledge and develop any new skills needed to meet their changing performance goals. This may or may not require additional development at the present time. Make this assessment as objectively as possible, and communicate it to your employees in a nonjudgmental way.

Fear of overextension Some employees simply do not wish to take on positions of greater responsibility within the organization. They are content at their level. Some may feel that they have already risen as high in the organization as they want to, or are able to, so they may wonder why they need to develop themselves or their skills at all. In this case, try to explain to the employee that development is about far more than just promotional opportunities. In reality, even if people remain in the same jobs, those jobs are constantly changing, and employees need to develop new skills so they can continue to meet the ever-changing requirements of their positions.

ASK THE EXPERTS

When I started to work out a development plan with one employee, she said, "I am really worried I won't have the time for this." She seems to have some flexibility in her schedule, so what is the real issue?

This employee is probably concerned that, rather than providing opportunities for growth, a development plan might just place another burden on her. Specifically, she may feel that she will be expected to invest lots of time in developing herself, or she may be worrying that she will be expected to take on many additional responsibilities or a heavier workload after she has completed additional training or development—without any raise in her salary or option for promotion. Reassure her that you are aware of, and sensitive to, her workload concerns. Go through her current schedule with her to see if she can fit in time for development and training without having to finish her regular work outside of working hours. If she does have some flexibility in her schedule, she might just need some help figuring out how to do her work more efficiently so she'll have extra time.

If she really does not have the time, then determine—as her manager—whether there are tasks she is performing that are less valuable to the organization than the development you want her to undertake. If the answer is yes, look for ways to shift some of those tasks elsewhere, either on a short-term or permanent basis. This may have the added effect of helping another employee to develop.

Managers' concerns

Sometimes it's the managers who resist the employee development process. They may feel that if they have hired the right person, then there is no need to develop new skills—especially if there is a steep learning curve for a skill. But the reality is that markets change rapidly and companies need to keep pace. That calls for swift responses. It may be quicker and more effective to develop the employees you have than to spend the time and money to recruit new ones.

Conversely, some managers worry that if they allow their employees to develop new skills, they may start looking for a new job outside the organization. While that is always a risk, by encouraging employees to grow within the organization, you can actually improve your chances of retaining them. Why? Because employees are far more likely to stay if managers are supportive of their growth within the organization. A lack of support may make them hesitant to even apply for internal opportunities—especially if your organization requires that internal applications be signed by their current manager. In such a situation, an employee may choose to look for a job outside the organization, rather than risk upsetting the manager.

Finally, of course, there is the issue of time. Managers have only so much time to work on developing their employees. But having a development plan in place can actually save you time in the long run, because it gets all the information out on the table in one meeting, rather than having it divided into impromptu talks. And it can save you the time—not to mention the expense—of looking for a new employee if the one you have now decides to leave because you did not support his or her continued growth.

"Setting performance goals with my employees was never a problem for me, but setting development goals was another story! I just didn't know—or, to be honest, understand—why I needed to worry about employees' own goals. I considered them to be personal, something for them to handle on their own time. Then, a few years ago, a friend of mine who's a supervisor at our West Coast office lost three top performers. They all said the same thing to her in their exit interviews: They wanted the chance to grow, and there just didn't seem to be any opportunities in their department. They wanted to get some more training, but there no was no scheduling flexibility. This was all I needed to hear to start creating development plans with my own employees. When one of our bookkeepers wanted to go back to school to get his accounting degree, I let him shift his schedule around to accommodate his classes. He's since gone on to become our top accountant and my right-hand man. Now I see how supporting my employees' development goals comes back to benefit not only them, but my organization—and me—as well."

Chloe A., Summit, NJ

Reality checks

When employees' goals just don't add up with reality

During the employee development meeting, you may learn that some of your employees have expectations or aspirations that are simply not realistic within your organization. For example, what do you do with one of your top sales assistants who tells you she wants to become an accountant? Employees obviously deserve the opportunity to pursue their dreams, but they also deserve to be given a realistic assessment of how likely it is that they can attain those goals at the expense of your organization. Companies can pay for only so much employee development. In some cases, organizations will not pay for training that is not strictly job-related. In other cases, employees may have to be told that their request for certain training is unrealistic given their job title and your company's policies. This is not always an easy conversation for managers to have with employees, but it is an important one.

Sometimes goals aren't realistic within your organization for reasons that have nothing to do with budgets, organizational policy, or tuition reimbursement. Whatever the reasons, your role is to give the employee an honest assessment of how realistic his goals are within your organization, not judge the merits of those goals. Then provide your employee with specific reasons why these goals are not realistic. Some possible reasons might be:

■ The time frame isn't consistent with what is reasonable to expect within your organization (for example, advancing from shift supervisor to operations vice president within two years).

■ The employee lacks the required qualifications, skills, or credentials required in your organization to perform the position (for example, a lunchroom monitor who wants to become vice principal).

■ There are a large number of highly qualified people competing for the position the employee is interested in training for.

COMMON TRAINING COURSES

Here is a list of the standard training classes offered by Fortune 500 companies—and by many smaller organizations too.

Time management
Software training
Performance appraisals
Team building
Marketing
Stress management
Leadership
Diversity
Conflict resolution

Employees can also enroll in privately offered workshops that cover these training topics and many more.

Helpful resources

Tools you can use

BOOKS

Bringing Out the Best in People
by Aubrey C. Daniels

The One Minute Manager
by Kenneth Blanchard, Ph.D.,
and Spencer Johnson, M.D.

*Leadership and the One Minute
Manager: Increasing Effectiveness
Through Situational Leadership*
by Kenneth Blanchard, Ph.D.,
and Patricia Zigarmi

1001 Ways to Reward Employees
by Bob Nelson

*Please Don't Just Do What I Tell
You, Do What Needs to Be Done:
Every Employee's Guide to Making
Work More Rewarding*
by Bob Nelson

WEB SITES

About.com: Human Resources
**http://humanresources.about.
com/library/blindexperfmgmt.
htm**
About.com's Performance Management,
Appraisal, and Evaluation Resources Web
site links to performance management and
appraisal sites.

About.com: Motivation
**http://humanresources.about.
com/cs/moralemotivation/**
About.com's Motivation-Morale-
Recognition-Rewards Web site directs you
to other useful sites relating to these all-
important management topics.

*About.com: Managing Day-to-Day
Performance*
**http://humanresources.about.
com/cs/manageperformance**
Offers links to lots of general sites
related to managing employees'
performance.

CHAPTER SIX

COMMON RATER ERRORS

Taking it personally

A good performance appraisal is a critical review of an employee. For new managers, the hard part of the process is being critical. Some managers overidentify with their employees, others fear their reactions, while some get blindsided by one or two outstanding characteristics and base their whole review on those characteristics. These errors in assessment, sometimes called **rater errors**, can cause managers to evaluate employees unfairly.

Before you start writing the performance appraisal, it's a good idea to be aware of the common mistakes that can befall managers, especially new ones. One type of rater error happens when managers *overidentify* with the job or employee they are trying to be objective about. In other words, managers become too subjective and lose their capacity to be critical. This can happen on a day-to-day basis, as well as at performance appraisal time. To overcome this error, you need to acknowledge your personal feelings about people who work for you (denying them only makes it worse) and then set those feelings aside as much as you can. Here are some common over identification rater errors:

The Similarity or "Just Like Me" Effect: It's only natural that people tend to gravitate toward others who share the same gender, age, race, religion, hobbies, interests, marital status, parental status, and so on. In your personal life, there's nothing wrong with bonding with those like you. At work, however, this can become a problem if you start rating certain employees higher than others just because you have things in common. The challenge becomes recognizing that this could be happening. How can you tell? If you find yourself excusing employees you like for not meeting their goals, then you may be falling into the similarity trap. A positive review is based on objective, observable, and measurable results, not on a gut feeling that this is a good employee who is doing a great job. Before you sign off on someone you "like," be sure you can provide objective examples of how they did—or did not—meet their goals and demonstrate competencies.

The Dissimilarity Effect: Just as people have a tendency to gravitate toward others who are like them, they also have a tendency to pull away from people who are different from them. When it comes to managing people, this kind of bias could result in your evaluating certain employees unfairly just because they are different from you. To counter this very human tendency, look for quantifiable information that will test your negative impression, not just confirm it. Don't let a negative "gut feeling" get in the way when it comes time to review results. The results should speak for themselves.

The "Benchmark" Effect: Sometimes managers use the rating they have earned from their own managers as the benchmark against which to measure their own employees' performance. For example, suppose that a manager earns an overall performance rating of "meets expectations." Suppose further that this manager views herself as an outstanding performer. This manager may then start to measure her employees' performance against her own performance—and rate them accordingly. In this case, "meets expectations" might become the highest rating that people reporting to this manager could receive, regardless of whether they exceed expectations. In the long run, this can demotivate the best employees, who may feel that no matter what they achieve, they will never earn a higher ratings.

NOTE: At the same time, be careful not to inflate ratings. Rating employees in the middle as "meeting expectations" is not like giving them a "C" grade. A rating of "exceeds expectations" requires a good deal of excellent work above the call of the job—and employees need to know this.

Fearing employees' reactions

A second category of rater error occurs when managers base their assessments of employees on how they think employees will perceive their evaluations. Being aware of employees' perceptions is appropriate, but being overly concerned with employees' reactions could taint your evaluation. In a sense, the manager is putting the employee in charge of the appraisal process. Again, the solution calls for you as a manager to acknowledge your fears and concerns and then turn your attention to the actual results of each employee. You want to focus on outcomes and behaviors, not personalities. Here's a closer look at these types of rater errors:

The Leniency Effect: Managers who make this error rate all of their employees generously. There are a number of reasons why managers might make this error. Some managers are concerned about doing anything that might demotivate their employees. Others are so reluctant to give their direct reports bad news that they will go to extremes to avoid it—even if it means being dishonest. Still other managers don't want their employees to think poorly of them, and think that their employees will work harder if they perceive the boss as being "nice." What these managers fail to understand, though, is that being fair is ultimately a lot more important than being nice. Giving your employees honest feedback is the only way they will get the info they need to bring their performance up to expected standards.

The Strictness Effect: Instead of being too generous in evaluating their employees, managers who make this mistake are overly strict. These managers don't worry about whether their employees think they are nice. Instead, these managers believe that employees may slack off if they are rated too highly. They may also believe that a lower rating will inspire their direct reports to strive for higher levels of achievement. In reality, however, consistently receiving a lower rating than what they actually earned can frustrate and demotivate employees. It may even motivate employees to look for a new job, working for a manager who is more fair.

The Central Tendency Effect: Some managers believe so strongly in team effort that they think giving employees differentiated ratings might undermine this team spirit. As a result, these managers tend to stick all of their employees in the middle of the performance rating scale. This can cause employees who have exceeded expectations to ask themselves, "Why should I keep working so hard if it's not even recognized?" Employees who know that they truly did not meet performance expectations may think, "Wow, I'm doing better than I thought. I was sure I would be told to bring my performance up a notch, but I guess I can just keep on doing what I'm doing." Finally, employees who are truly meeting expectations may feel as though they are being evaluated accurately, but may be perplexed if they find out that their colleagues were rated the same way, despite their performance. This can ultimately lead them to believe you are not evaluating anyone accurately, and that you are not a fair manager.

The Contrast Effect: This rater error happens when managers compare direct reports against each other instead of judging them based on objective results. This can result in employees being rated higher or lower than they would normally have been if the manager were using objective standards. To avoid this rater error, try not to compare the performances of employees in your group. Employees are individuals and deserve to be reviewed on their own merits, not on whether they are better or worse than their peers.

Overgeneralizing

Another type of rater error occurs when managers allow a single dimension of an employee's performance to affect the overall assessment. This takes two forms: generalizing performance in an overly positive way, and generalizing it in an overly negative way.

The Halo Effect: Sometimes a manager may be unduly influenced by one outstanding area of performance. For example, you may have one employee who is superb at landing new business. His only problem is that he sometimes confuses customers' orders. You ignore this inattention to detail (which actually has lost you some business) because you are so impressed with his sales ability. But if you let your assessment of this employee be determined solely by the fact that he is an outstanding salesman, you may experience the halo effect—viewing an employee as an "angel" because of this one characteristic and ignoring any performance problems. To avoid this, always make sure to consider every dimension of performance separately. In this case, the employee should be evaluated not just on his sales, but on his follow-through, such as his attention to detail, among other things.

The Horns Effect: This is the opposite of the halo effect. Here you let a single negative component of performance affect the entire evaluation. Imagine you have one employee who gets new accounts, but forgets to write up new orders, or if he does, makes errors in his paperwork so that the orders are inaccurate. If you allow your evaluation of this employee to be determined primarily by this one factor, inattention to detail, you could experience the horns effect. That's not to say that this one particular factor is not important—it could even be the most important factor to some managers. But it can't be the only important one, and you need to evaluate every area of performance separately.

ASK THE EXPERTS

I have an employee who is great at his work, but is always complaining about his salary. Is this a personal issue I should take up with him? Or is this a work issue that I should raise in his performance review?

Any and all job-related concerns should be addressed with employees as soon as possible. Concerns about pay definitely fall into this category. Rather than waiting until the performance appraisal, speak with this employee when he first brings up this concern. If this employee creates problems in the workplace by voicing frequent public complaints, move quickly to correct this disruptive behavior.

My boss is very keen on one of my direct reports and feels that we should promote her right after this round of performance appraisals. I have some serious reservations about her work. Should I tell my boss about them before I do her performance review?

Sometimes senior management falls prey to the "halo effect" (see page 100). It sounds like this may be happening to your boss. So, yes, it's important to give your boss a fair and complete assessment of this employee's performance—in objective, measurable, and observable terms—so that your boss won't be surprised by your review of this employee after the fact. And always make sure the feedback is going both ways: Employees must get this regularly from you, and you need to provide it regularly to them and to your boss.

Focusing on recent work

The recency effect

There is one more type of common error that you need to look out for. This occurs when you let an employee's recent behavior overwhelmingly shape your evaluation of his or her performance for the entire appraisal period. This is where having a performance management system in place is invaluable.

The Recency Effect: Right before the end of the performance management period, a phenomenon can take place in which employees, believing that managers are paying closer attention to their performance, put themselves on their best behavior. The reality is that, in many cases, these employees are smart to do this: Lots of managers do pay more attention at this time, and this can lead to the rater error known as the recency effect, in which managers base their evaluations on only this short period of recent good behavior. How can you avoid this common pitfall? By including behaviors and results from the entire year, preferably all four quarters. If you are missing information because you are new on the job as a manager, then ask previous managers for their feedback. Your goal is to make sure that the performance appraisals you prepare reflect employees' performance over the entire measurement period, and make note of specific behaviors you have observed throughout the year, not just at the end.

"Before I really understood performance appraisals, I didn't even realize I was making mistakes when I evaluated my employees. When I did their appraisals, I used to compare them to each other instead of to the job requirements—which I later learned is called "the contrast effect." As part of this, I also used "friendly competition" to try to motivate my employees, and would post lists of the highest producers to the lowest producers. Then something happened that made me realize how wrong my methods were. After the last performance appraisal period, the employee who was always at the bottom of my list came to talk to me. He was upset because even though he had exceeded all of his performance standards, he was still at the bottom of the heap. He wanted to quit and couldn't understand why I was humiliating him. I thought about it some, and realized he was right. I was trying so hard to get my employees to outdo each other that I didn't recognize it when they met their own goals. So I replaced this system with one in which I recognize all employees who have met or exceeded performance standards—regardless of how the employees compare to each other. This carries over into how I do the appraisals now, and keeps me from comparing employees with each other when I complete their performance appraisal forms."

Philicia R., Beverly, MA

Helpful resources

Tools you can use

BOOKS

Effective Phrases for Performance Appraisals: A Guide to Successful Evaluations
by James E. Neal Jr.

Peak Performance, Aligning the Hearts and Minds of Your Employees
by Jon Katzenbach

Performance Management
by Robert Bacal

Powerful Performance Appraisals: How to Set Expectations and Work Together to Improve Performance
by Karen McKirchy

WEB SITES

Performance Management Homepage
www.p-management.com
Provides useful links and suggested readings on feedback and other performance management topics.

CHAPTER SEVEN

SELF-APPRAISALS

Using self-appraisals

In many companies, employees are required to assess their perform-ance during the measurement period by filling in self-appraisal forms. This is perhaps the most direct way of getting employees involved in the appraisal process, by providing a simple fill-in-the-blanks structure that lets employees reveal how they feel about the work they accomplished over the past year.

Self-appraisals can be a valuable tool for managers, reminding them of accomplishments they may have accidentally overlooked. They also allow managers to correct any misinformation before the performance appraisal is set in stone. Plus, managers can gain a lot of insight into the employee's viewpoints and concerns. This knowledge of where employees' perceptions may differ from your perceptions will also help you prepare for the actual appraisal meeting, so that you aren't sur-prised by the employee's perspective on his or her own performance.

NOTE: If you find self-appraisals to be beneficial and your company doesn't require them, you might want to consider adding this step to your performance appraisal process. This may require coming up with a form (which can look almost exactly like the performance appraisal form you will use) and getting approval from your HR department. (See page 109 for a typical form.)

ASK THE EXPERTS

Should I wait to start working on my employees' performance appraisals until I get their self-appraisals back?

This is not recommended by management experts, although it is common. Some managers do this because they think that using their employees' self-appraisals as the basis of their performance reviews saves them time and energy. But beware that this can lead to problems in objectivity. As a manager, you should base your initial assessment of each aspect of the employee's performance on what you have observed and measured. If you let the employee self-appraisal lead the way, you can open yourself up for errors, especially if any of your employees has an unrealistic view of how well he or she performed.

I have one employee who is late with his self-appraisal. It is now holding up the whole process. I've told him repeatedly to get it done, but he keeps stalling. What should I do?

Of course, doing a self-appraisal does require some effort. But if your employee is truly pressed for time, it may help for you to review his workload and see if he is really unable to spare the hour to two it would take to fill in a self-appraisal form. If you think your employee is worried about the whole process, then remind him that he has done a lot of good work all year long, and doing a little bit more now is the best way of making sure that he will get credit for all that work. Explain that the form is just a summary of what has taken place during the year, and have him review copies of memos or e-mails from throughout the year to jog his memory.

The self-appraisal form

Short and sweet wins the day

There are various types of self-appraisal forms, but whatever form your company uses, it should be customized to reflect your department's particular type of work and objectives as they relate to employees' job duties. In other words, if you manage salespeople who work on commission, it might be helpful if the self-appraisal form had a section on selling ability, while if you run a computer repair service, it might be useful to have a self-rating category on technical expertise. This will usually coincide with the categories on the actual performance appraisal form.

In fact, all of the major sections on a self-appraisal form should complement the categories on the performance appraisal form the manager uses. For the manager, this streamlines the process of comparing an employee's self-appraisal with his own first draft. If the categories on each form are not comparable, there is no common ground for a manager and an employee to discuss the employee's performance.

If you are setting up a performance appraisal system, know that most performance appraisal software programs include sample appraisal forms that you can alter to fit your requirements. You can also use a manager's appraisal form as a template, removing the final rating sections and altering other sections as necessary.

SELF-APPRAISAL FORM
(Short Form)

Company Name _____

Employee's name _____

Job title _____

Date of hire _____

Supervisor's name _____

Department _____

■ Review your job performance as it relates to your job description and the goals that were set for 2003 and/or at your last performance appraisal.
■ Identify specific examples of significant accomplishments and areas of needed improvement.

Significant accomplishments:
_____
_____
_____

Progress toward goals:
_____
_____
_____

Developmental needs:
_____
_____
_____

Your concerns

While the benefits of self-appraisal may seem obvious, not all managers are convinced that it's a good idea. This hesitancy may have less to do with reality and more to do with myths, misconceptions, and misunderstandings that can cause managers to fear this process. As with any misconception, the best way to deal with it is to face it directly. So take a look at the top two myths about self-appraisals in more detail:

Myth #1: Employees won't view their work accurately. Some managers fear employees will puff up their accomplishments over the year. While it's true that some employees may do this, the opposite actually happens more often: Many employees evaluate their performance more harshly than their managers do. Why? Often, employees are trying so hard not to be perceived as going easy on themselves that they deliberately review their work harshly. They may prefer hearing their manager say "You did much better than this" to hearing their manager say "Sorry, but you didn't perform as well as you think you did."

Myth #2: Employees will develop unrealistic notions about their performance which you will have to work to dispel. Managers who believe in this myth are concerned that employees can become too insistent on their own appraisal of themselves and become inflexible if the manager disagrees with them. Yes, chances are that you may have to spend some time working through your different perspectives, but that can only be for the better in the long run. For starters, help your employees understand that self-appraisal is one tool—though not the only tool—that they can use to help improve their performance and to let their boss know how they feel about their job responsibilities and workload.

Employees' concerns

By now you're probably convinced of the value of self-appraisals. But what if your employees are not? When you meet with employees to discuss the self-appraisal, encourage them to be honest about their concerns. These worries can take several forms, so prepare yourself now to address these common concerns:

"Isn't this *your* job?" Some employees may feel that completing the self-appraisal means that they're doing their manager's job for him or her. (And if the manager doesn't prepare the first draft of the appraisal before looking at the employee's self-appraisal, this might be true, and could greatly diminish the manager's credibility.) The best way to work around this concern is to explain to employees that you are writing appraisals for each employee—often much longer ones.

"I don't have time for this." Employees may feel that by being asked to prepare a self-appraisal they are being forced to do extra work. This won't be as likely to happen if you communicate clearly with them about how the process works. Explain that preparing a self-appraisal is, in fact, an important duty of their job. If the employee still says that he or she doesn't have enough time, set a later deadline, if possible, or review his or her workload. If the employee is right, rearrange assignments and/or deadlines so that the employee has ample time to complete the self-appraisal during regular working hours. Don't expect employees to complete it at home or during nonwork hours.

"What's in it for me?" Employees may worry that they may not reap any benefits from the effort put into doing a self-appraisal. If you have employees who feel this way, explain to them that they will benefit from this process, partly because the self-appraisal process provides a great way for them to discuss concerns they may not have mentioned before. Assure them that everything they tell you in the appraisal will be taken into consideration, and that during the actual performance appraisal meeting, you will be willing to revisit any items that the employee raised on the self-appraisal that remain unresolved.

"Why do I have to do this? No one else has to." Employees may resist completing the self-appraisal if it's not an organization-wide initiative. In this case, the challenge is to explain to employees that the self-appraisal is a showcase for their accomplishments and a chance to air their concerns and have them taken seriously.

"I'm a terrible writer. I'll only make myself look bad." If writing is not a major component of an employee's job, she might feel that she is being asked to do something she is not skilled at, and may worry that she will be judged on her writing skills. In this case, assure her that it's not necessary to write at length; even just listing specific accomplishments will help. And remind nervous employees that how they write their self-appraisal won't impact the rating they earn from you, and that you are there to support them if they need help.

Interpreting self-appraisals

Using them to inform your appraisal

Great—you've gotten all the forms back from your employees. Now what? As with everything else related to the performance appraisal process, the key is to take it step by step:

Step 1: Review. Compare the self-appraisal to the first draft of the appraisal you wrote. If you haven't done a first draft, then compare the appraisal to the file you have been keeping on that employee (see page 30). Pay close attention to the specific comments and examples that the employee has provided for each section of the form. Try to ignore any strong superlatives or overly modest language—pare these away and focus primarily on the performance described, goals achieved, specific examples mentioned. And be on the lookout for sidelong comments about the workplace, coworkers, or your management style—these can be very revealing, and can help you learn more about what needs to be improved in your organization, but remember that you may have to read between the lines.

Step 2: Check any discrepancies. Ask yourself if the information seems accurate. Is your employee's version of his or her accomplishments in line with your take on them? If not, investigate these differences. Look through your files for any documentation that will help clarify the issue. Ask other managers for feedback. And, perhaps most important, go back through all of the notes you have made throughout the year, as well as any documentation from feedback discussions.

Step 3: Reconcile. Resolve the discrepancies as best you can. Simply state the objective accomplishments as you see them and ignore the errors you found in the self-appraisal. When you show your appraisal to your employees, they can choose to raise discrepancies or not. They may have material that supports them; if that is the case, then ask to see it. If not, then refer to the objective facts. However, do note that the final appraisal should not reflect a compromise between the two versions, but a real and genuine accounting of the truth.

Step 4: Interpret the self-appraisal. Use self-appraisals to help inform your objective assessment about your employees. (See chapter 6 for common assessment errors.) Your goal is to use this information to help you steer toward a more accurate, helpful performance appraisal. However, this is easier said than done. Here are two common misinterpretations:

If an employee's self-evaluation is a lot lower than mine, I should adjust my performance appraisal downward.

Not necessarily. You should only do this if the employee's assessment of his or her own performance is accurate. Self-appraisals sometimes become a reflection of how employees feel about themselves in general, instead of an objective assessment of their performance during a particular measurement period. People who don't view themselves positively may reflect that perception in their self-appraisals. To find out the truth, you'll need to do the research. As always, your goal should be to evaluate objectively the details of employees' performance, steering clear of assessing their personalities, attitudes, or how they—or you—feel about them personally. If this means your appraisal ends up more positive than your employee's self-appraisal, that doesn't mean you're a "softie"—it just means you haven't let any biases impact your assessment.

If there are serious discrepancies between an employee's self-appraisal and my appraisal, I should talk to him or her before preparing the final draft.

It's better to resist the temptation to talk with your employees about any differences between the two forms before you prepare your final draft and hold the appraisal meeting, because any issues should always be addressed in the context of the appraisal. Instead, when you explain the self-appraisal process, assure your employees that the two of you will have a chance to discuss any differences between the forms during the appraisal meeting. Then do the research to see if you can reconcile these differences (see page 116).

Reconciling differences

While most employee self-appraisals go pretty smoothly, every now and then managers will hit a bump in the road. But don't let that worry you. If you find yourself in the following situations, know that there is a graceful (and fair) way to solve the problem:

Situation #1: "I've checked my files and my employee's self-appraisal overly glorifies his actual achievements." If this happens, look on it as a learning opportunity—one that you can put to immediate use. If the information in the employee's self-appraisal is grandiose, you won't be surprised then when that attitude spills out during the performance appraisal meeting. You now have time to prepare an accurate appraisal and to strategize about how to discuss the differing degrees of glory at the appraisal meeting.

Situation #2: "My employee's self-appraisal contains things that I know are not true." You have the responsibility to write a performance appraisal that communicates truthful assessments, even if your version of the truth is very different from the employee's version of it. As long as you can support your version of the truth with specifics, you should be fine. When it's time to communicate this to the employee during the performance appraisal meeting, you can make this difficult conversation go as smoothly as possible by sticking to objective facts, namely, this employee's actual results.

WHAT IF?

One employee's self-appraisal was really sloppily and poorly written. Do I take this into account when evaluating his performance and writing my final draft of his appraisal?

No. It's important not to let yourself be influenced by how well—or how poorly—employees have written their self-appraisals. Even if writing well is a skill required for an employee's job, focus your assessment on how he writes for his job, not how well he wrote his self-appraisal. This can be challenging, especially if the employee is a talented, persuasive writer. So make a concerted effort to gauge and manage your reactions against the requirements of the position. After all, the employee may have been nervous about writing the appraisal, pressed for time, or confused about the directions. During the meeting, you may find out if any of these things may have affected the quality of his self-appraisal.

There are two minor discrepancies between my employee's self-appraisal and my appraisal. Can I bring them up during her appraisal meeting instead of checking them out first?

It's probably not a wise idea. It is better to take some time and check into these discrepancies before your formal meeting. Why? Because you don't want these minor differences to overshadow your meeting. Checking out these minor concerns will show your concern and care, and will have a major impact on the quality and tone of the conversations you will have with your employee during the meeting. These steps will also have an impact on how she views the whole performance appraisal process, so this is where you really need to do the work to show her that what she thinks matters to you and that you take her input seriously—even if, in the end, you don't agree with her assessment of her performance.

Helpful resources

Tools you can use

BOOKS

Powerful Performance Appraisals: How to Set Expectations and Work Together to Improve Performance by Karen McKirchy

Effective Phrases for Performance Appraisals: A Guide to Successful Evaluations by James E. Neal, Jr.

Performance Appraisal: State of the Art in Practice by James W. Smither

WEB SITES

eCornell
www.eCornell.com/catalog/ne/ ilrmd511.jsp
Cornell University offers an online course, called "Managing Performance," that presents a collaborative approach to feedback, goal setting, and appraisal.

Watson Wyatt
www.WatsonWyatt.com
Watson Wyatt's Organizational Effectiveness practice specializes in helping organizations develop their coaching and leadership capabilities.

CHAPTER EIGHT

POWERFUL APPRAISAL LANGUAGE

The language of appraisals

Choose your words carefully for maximum impact

Although most appraisal forms have a rating system, it's the language you use on that form that creates an overall impression of an employee, and helps that employee to understand what you really think of his or her performance. The more precise your language is, the more valuable the feedback will be to the employee. That's why it's so important to choose your words wisely and to be as descriptive and exact as you possibly can.

Avoid bland adjectives, such as "good," or vague phrases such as "nice effort" or "fine performance," and instead try to use active, detailed descriptions that speak exactly to the competency you are rating. For example, instead of using the vague phrase "works well with others" to describe an employee's talent for maximizing the different skills of team members, use a more powerful, exact phrase, such as "makes maximum use of the diverse talents of team members." Follow this with examples of this behavior—these examples are even more important than the words you use to describe performance. Then note the effect this talent had on the organization and on other employees.

Even if you're not the world's most gifted writer, choosing the right words for the appraisal form is not an impossible task. A thesaurus may come in handy, and over time, you will probably develop your own "mini-dictionary" or vocabulary list of useful phrases that reflect the unique culture and goals of your organization.

QUALIFYING YOUR DESCRIPTIONS

Not only should the language you use vary by the job function you are describing, it should also vary according to your assessment of whether an employee's behavior exceeds, meets, or does not meet expectations. So, while you may quickly acquire some stock phrases for appraisal forms, it's good to know how to qualify these phrases based on performance.

This is where a collection of helpful verbs, adjectives, and adverbs comes in handy. By using these to modify a stock phrase, you can convey a great deal about an employee's level of accomplishment. And by adding "not" before an adjective, or adding the prefix "un," you can change the word into a less positive assessment if necessary—or look up antonyms in a dictionary for this. Some basic examples:

Adjectives	Adverbs	Verbs
authoritative	extremely	accentuates
masterful	favorably	assimilates
dependable	consistently	augments
unrivaled	effectively	contributes
superior	successfully	demonstrates
competent	powerfully	displays
efficient	accurately	encourages
extraordinary	regularly	insures
impeccable	completely	maximizes
meticulous	concisely	produces
progressive	industriously	refines
remarkable	meaningfully	stimulates
unique	properly	supports
exceptional	realistically	surmounts
outstanding	strongly	sustains
profound	vigorously	utilizes

Knowledge

This is often the most general description on an appraisal form, and it usually pertains to employees' basic comprehension of their jobs and their professional field.

Following are some key phrases you can use to describe an employee who meets expectations in these various areas. (Remember, you can alter these to reflect different levels of performance; see page 121.)

Professional knowledge

- Displays competent level of job skills
- Demonstrates a functional knowledge of job requirements
- Has solid comprehension of the field
- Stays informed of latest developments in the field and the organization

Technical knowledge

- Can competently use all required software (or equipment)
- Demonstrates comprehensive technical skills
- Skilled at trouble-shooting and solving technical glitches
- Uses the latest techniques and equipment to reduce costs and increase competitiveness

Competency

- Follows directions efficiently and well
- Adapts quickly to new requirements and procedures
- Shows good self-perception of abilities
- Consistently works to sharpen skills

Accuracy

- Balances need for accuracy with speed
- Consistently maintains accuracy under pressure or deadline
- Displays meticulous attention to detail
- Strives for perfection, but balances that with realistic assessment of tasks

INTELLECTUAL SKILLS

Intellectual skills refers to an employee's basic level of comprehension and general analytical abilities. Useful phrases to describe an employee who shows good mental agility on the job include:

- Demonstrates a high level of concentration and focus
- Consistently alert, quick, and responsive
- Displays fresh insights and comes up with innovative approaches
- Shows considerable mental flexibility
- Competent in both theoretical and practical thinking
- Shows keen comprehension, retention, and recall
- Has a high level of intellectual inquisitiveness
- Possesses good analytical skills

Cost management

Cost management is a fairly straightforward area to evaluate. Generally speaking, it's pretty easy to figure out if employees are able to manage or cut costs and allocate resources effectively simply by reviewing the financial information related to the employee's performance. Evaluating cost-management skills is made even easier if, at the beginning of the performance management period, you work with the employee to establish measurable financial goals. For example, if an employee's goal is to reduce costs in his department by 3% over the year, it is pretty easy to determine whether or not he met that goal simply by going over his department's financial records for the year.

This area of performance is also related to efficiency and productivity, since an efficient and productive employee is one who will save your organization money.

Following are some helpful phrases you can use to describe an employee who is meeting his or her cost-management goals:

General cost-management skills
- Makes adequate use of allocated funds and resources
- Efficiently manages departmental budget
- Develops and implements cost-saving techniques
- Consistently controls expenses without sacrificing quality

Efficiency

- Produces lasting results with a minimum of supervision
- Shows good ability to achieve results quickly and accurately
- Encourages and demonstrates high level of efficiency and effectiveness
- Simplifies systems effectively and reduces unnecessary paperwork

Productivity

- Resolves problems that interfere with productivity
- Regularly produces beyond expectations
- Contributes substantially to the growth and operation of the company
- Consistently meets production goals without sacrificing quality

Motivation

Looking closely at an employee's drive and commitment

Evaluating an employee's level of motivation can be somewhat tricky. On the one hand, it's not a concrete skill, like cost-management ability. On the other hand, it's absolutely central to good performance; an employee who is not motivated to succeed will simply not perform up to speed.

The best way to get a handle on this area is to pay attention to how employees behave as they go about their work. Assuming that their jobs provide enough incentive and challenge to motivate them to succeed, what kind of commitment and drive do they exhibit on a daily basis? Although you obviously don't want to evaluate an employee solely on these sets of behaviors, they are important factors. Just be sure when evaluating motivation that you do not let your personal feelings about the employee muddy the waters. To stay as objective as possible, always relate evidence of motivation to concrete accomplishments.

Here are some phrases to describe highly motivated employees:

Motivation

- Highly performance conscious
- Displays a strong sense of purpose
- Capable of sustained commitment to tasks
- Has keen incentive to succeed
- Sets and reaches ever-higher goals and expectations
- Exhibits strong competitive drive
- Maintains high level of energy and enthusiasm for work
- Is a consistent self-starter
- Encourages determination and desire to achieve in others

ASK THE EXPERTS

On the appraisal form, what is the best way to describe and rate an employee who is consistently one of our top three sellers, and yet is known for being discourteous to customers on occasion?

These are separate behaviors and need to be evaluated separately. Address employees' accomplishments with respect to sales in the appropriate goals section, then address lack of courtesy to customers in the appropriate competency section.

SALES LEADERSHIP

For sales-related jobs, sales leadership ability is one way that motivation may manifest itself. Sales leadership describes an employee's ability to deal proactively with customers and competitors, as well as to inspire other sales team members to achieve top results. In an appraisal, an employee who demonstrates good sales leadership skills might be described in the following ways:

- Successfully employs organization's preferred sales strategies
- Displays deep understanding of general sales philosophy
- Responds constructively to customer wants and needs
- Deals promptly and effectively with customer complaints
- Serves as a role model for other salespeople on staff
- Responds decisively to changing sales environment
- Researches and keeps abreast of competitors' sales strategies and results
- Is courteous and professional in all sales contexts
- Makes full use of market research to set and reach sales goals

Communication

Employees who deal with the public obviously need to have superior communication skills, but these skills are also necessary to insure that information flows freely and constructively inside your organization. Good communication requires a broad range of skills, from writing and verbal ability to the talent for making powerful presentations.

Here are some sample phrases to describe employees with a good grasp of basic communication principles:

General communication skills
- Enhances effectiveness of communications by coworkers
- Facilitates meetings that accomplish objectives
- Encourages open and regular communication within organization
- Regularly updates staff on developments that affect them

Writing skills
- Writes clearly, effectively, and concisely
- Converts complex materials into easily understood format
- Displays solid knowledge of grammar and punctuation

Verbal skills
- Articulate, thoughtful, and concise speaker
- Comfortable interacting verbally with employees at all levels
- Efficiently explains complex ideas and procedures

Presentation skills

- Easily gains respect and attention of audience

- Organizes and presents ideas clearly

- Creates powerful, focused presentations that further the company's goals

Customer service skills

- Builds and maintains a loyal customer following

- Displays tact and courtesy when under pressure from clients

- Relates well to customers from all backgrounds

- Follows directions without needing repeated clarification

- Accurately and quickly comprehends all types of requests

- Always asks questions when something is not understood

Dependability

Dependable employees—those who can always be counted on to go the extra mile to make a deadline, and whom you trust to always perform at a high level—make up the backbone of most organizations. And though praising this quality may not make employees glow as much as praising their innovative or visionary contributions, most do recognize that dependability is at the heart of their value as an employee, and know it's one of the main things a future employer will look for. So make sure to evaluate dependability in as much detail as possible on the appraisal form, covering not only basic issues, such as whether an employee shows up for work on time, but an employee's professionalism, ethical behavior, and level of cooperation.

Some phrases to describe dependable employees:

General dependability

- Industrious, accurate, and conscientious in performing tasks
- Accepts responsibility for completing projects without hesitation
- Regularly attains fine results, even with limited resources
- Consistently delivers on promises and meets deadlines

Responsibility

- Willingly takes full responsibility for own decisions
- Enthusiastic about taking on challenging assignments
- Demonstrates high level of professional maturity
- Views new assignments as opportunity for growth and expansion of responsibilities

Reliability

- Can always be counted on to pitch in when extra help is needed
- Work consistently exhibits high level of achievement
- Requires little to no supervision or reminders to complete projects
- Sets and maintains high standards for self and coworkers
- Maintains excellent record of attendance and punctuality

Problem solving

As much as managers may wish for all employees to be successful problem solvers, it's best to be realistic when evaluating this ability. Problem-solving is not the easiest skill to pick up, and many employees are satisfied with supporting the work of others who come up with the solutions. That's why an employee who shows good problem-solving skills is such an asset to your organization, and should be praised accordingly.

At the same time, if your organization or a particular position requires a high level of problem-solving ability, and an employee does not display this, it's something you definitely need to point out in the appraisal and discuss with the employee. Then, follow up by giving employees opportunities to improve their problem-solving skills by taking on new challenges. This can result not only in a higher level of work, but in a more satisfied and motivated employee.

These sample phrases should help inspire you when describing an employee with solid problem-solving skills:

General problem-solving ability
- Skillful in identifying, analyzing, and solving problems
- Comes up with creative and cost-effective solutions
- Creates far-reaching solutions that benefit the entire organization
- Always concentrates on resolving problems in the early stages
- Skillful in resolving the underlying issues around a problem—not just the symptoms
- Treats problems as opportunities for growth and leadership

Time management

- Effectively allocates and manages personal time resources
- Delegates tasks in order to maximize time management
- Continuously strives to "work smarter, not harder"
- Comes up with creative and effective methods for accomplishing more in less time

Resourcefulness

- Manages limited resources effectively to get a good return on investment
- Displays self-reliance and strength in stressful situations
- Takes creative and organized approach to allocating resources
- Makes excellent use of available information and resources from Internet, other media, and/or industry associations

Planning

Well-organized employees are always an asset to an organization—especially if they are able to organize not just their time and priorities, but also the time and priorities of others. In a dynamic, growing organization where multitasking is essential, an employee who shows good prioritizing and organizational skills can make or break important projects or goals. Therefore, make sure to recognize employees who show good planning skills, and if they are exceptionally talented at this, see if you can find out during the appraisal meeting what their tricks are—then share them with other employees. Or even better, arrange to have this employee train others in these skills.

Some ways to describe an employee with good planning ability:

Prioritizing

- Prioritizes goals and tasks when faced with competing requests, deadlines, and demands
- Concentrates on priorities with greatest payback potential
- Excels in eliminating trivial tasks and those that contribute least to organizational goals
- Sets and achieves goals on deadline without wasting time, energy, and essential resources
- Focuses well on both long-term and short-term planning needs

Organizing

- Excels in promoting productivity of team
- Identifies and fills organizational needs, even when under stress
- Style of work consistently builds organizational effectiveness
- Makes effective use of organizing tools (calendars, PDAs, to-do lists, etc.)

Project management

- Successfully juggles multiple projects
- Committed to completing projects successfully
- Shows keen attention to project details without forgetting larger picture
- Sets project goals with ease and manages resources for reaching them

QUALITY MANAGEMENT

How are quality management skills related to planning and prioritizing skills? An employee who displays good quality management understands how to prioritize the quality needs of your product or organization. Such an employee knows which aspects of quality are most crucial, and which ones are minor or would waste time if allowed to become central issues. Some quality management phrases that you might use on an appraisal form (and might back up with actual quality measurements or figures):

- Consistently meets goals for cutting costs and improving quality of outputs
- Constantly analyzes and improves production processes
- Works hard to lower defect or return rate of products
- Can accurately prioritize quality and cost requirements
- Delivers accurate and timely work to management and clients

Adaptability

In today's shifting economic climate, organizations need to be highly flexible so they can cope with—and even profit from—sudden changes in the market. The same goes for employees. Long gone are the days when they spent their whole lives working in one career or industry and for one employer. To take advantage of the dynamics of the current labor landscape, today's employees need to be able to adapt quickly to changing conditions in their jobs and companies—not to mention roll with changes in their industries.

In the workplace, employees who display these attributes might be described on performance appraisal forms with these kinds of phrases:

Adaptability

- Flexibly and effectively responds to challenging situations
- Gracefully accepts feedback on changes to goals and priorities
- Willing to take on and complete unfamiliar tasks
- Always willing to work unusual or extra hours if needed

Flexibility

- Easily accommodates changes in procedures or instructions
- Accepts changes to work routine without becoming agitated
- Adapts to changing requirements with a minimum of supervision
- Accommodates and balances needs of all levels of staff
with own priorities and tasks

COPING WITH STRESS

One important aspect of flexibility is the ability to cope with stress. An employee who can remain relaxed and level-headed during periods of high demand or workplace conflict and change is particularly valuable to an organization. Such an employee can continue to produce under stress, and may also help calm down other employees, allowing them to continue producing as well. This kind of stress-resistant employee might be described in performance appraisals in the following ways:

- Always remains calm and collected, even in high-anxiety situations
- Never loses temper or raises voice when provoked by colleagues or clients
- Copes gracefully with multiple demands from managers and coworkers
- Stays focused and performs well under deadline
- Manages crises, risks, uncertainty, and unexpected situations with ease

Creativity

A quality that your employees need to make a difference

Like judging an employee's level of motivation, evaluating creative ability can be a little harder than evaluating something like dependability, just because there aren't familiar handholds like punctuality to consider. What you do have to consider is an employee's approach to problems or projects. Does the employee come up with innovative and successful solutions that stand apart from others' ideas? Other components of creativity include vision and initiative. An employee with vision is able to imagine and project long-term solutions and also understand your core mission. Likewise, an employee with initiative takes the reins easily and seeks out new opportunities and resources. Such employees often come up with creative ways to maximize these opportunities without being told.

If you have a creative employee, you have a powerful weapon against your competitors; creative solutions can set your organization apart from the crowd. Some ways to describe a creative employee:

Creativity
- Possesses imaginative insight
- Develops and implements creative strategies and alternatives
- Is able to easily adjust and optimize work flow
- Fosters an environment for creative expression and problem solving

Vision
- Has deep understanding of organization's mission
- Supports and encourages expression of management's vision
- Displays visionary leadership qualities
- Exhibits visionary thinking when formulating long-term goals

Initiative

- Demonstrates self-reliance and ability to self-direct

- Takes action in appropriate and timely manner

- Seizes new opportunities with enthusiasm

- Identifies and makes good use of new ideas, techniques, and approaches

ASK THE EXPERTS

Even though creativity is a big category on our appraisal forms, I don't understand how I can rate it. Creativity seems like a talent you are either born with or you're not, so how can I evaluate employees on this—not to mention assign a numerical rating?

If your form requires you to rate a competency like creativity, try to think about it not in terms of its dictionary definition, but in terms of the particular activities or behaviors that define it in your organization. Ask yourself: Do the outputs which employees have produced—e.g., ways of doing their jobs, projects or tasks they have completed—show originality and vision? These kinds of specific examples of behavior are much easier to rate. By evaluating employees' performance in relation to this talent, you'll avoid having to judge whether they are inherently creative people. And when you think about it that way, it doesn't even matter whether an employee was "born creative"; instead, what matters is how and if this employee has used that ability in concrete ways in the workplace.

Team skills

Sports metaphors are often used to describe the corporate world, and for good reason: An organization that functions smoothly, like a baseball team with players who are always in sync, is the result of good teamwork. In order for your organization to run like a well-honed sports team, employees need to be able to work together and play off of one another's strengths. Those who cannot work well on a team can easily throw a wrench into the system, and their good ideas can disappear into a vacuum. If you have employees who work well together on a team, make sure to recognize them for this skill, and encourage them to help bring "lone wolf" employees into the fold.

These phrases might be used to describe team players and those who show good management skills:

Team skills

- Identifies and utilizes strengths of individual team members
- Builds teams of people with complementary skills
- Understands and promotes team objectives
- Skillfully allocates and utilizes team resources

Management ability

- Organizes people and resources for greatest success
- Effective at managing and defusing employee conflicts
- Leadership effectiveness encourages employees' best work
- Takes responsibility for developing skills and encouraging achievements of staff
- Understands and applies contemporary management techniques

- Conveys importance of individual responsibility and accountability to direct reports
- Is well respected by direct reports for superior management skills
- Evaluates and improves own management techniques
- Does not micromanage, nor manage from a distance
- Sets standards for direct reports in terms of professionalism and dedication
- Implements changes effectively and with enthusiasm

ASK THE EXPERTS

I have an employee who is more than eager to sign up for project teams, but then rarely contributes anything. On the appraisal form, how should I praise her great enthusiasm, while also gently urging her to contribute more?

Even though they both relate to teamwork, these are two different kinds of behaviors that need to be evaluated and described separately. Volunteering is a positive behavior, so communicate this on the form with positive descriptive phrases that draw on concrete examples. But since contributing to the team is an aspect of her performance that needs improvement, be sure to point this out, too—also listing specific examples. By listing actual instances of when this employee served on a team but did not contribute much, you will give weight to your evaluation, and the employee will be able to focus on those specific examples and ask herself why she did not contribute. This should hopefully back up any constructive feedback (see page 206) you've given her.

Helpful resources

Tools you can use

BOOKS

The Performance Management Activity Pack: Tools for Building Appraisal and Performance Development Skills
by Terry Gillen

Manage People, Not Personnel: Motivation and Performance Appraisal (Harvard Business Review Book Series)
by Victor H. Vroom

Performance Appraisal Phrase Book: Effective Words, Phrases, and Techniques for Successful Evaluations
by Corey Sandler and Janice Keefe

Perfect Phrases for Performance Reviews : Hundreds of Ready-to-Use Phrases That Describe Your Employees' Performance
by Douglas Max and Robert Bacal

WEB SITES

Performance Appraisal   Tips Page
http://iso9k1.home.att.net/pa/ performance_appraisal.html
A performance appraisal tips page by Dexter Hansen.

About.com: Human Resources
http://humanresources.about.com /library/blindexperfmgmt.htm
Performance management, appraisal, and evaluation resources at About.com.

CHAPTER NINE

WRITING THE APPRAISAL

Build your confidence

You don't need to be a novelist to write a good first draft

So you're ready to fill out the actual performance appraisal form. Take a deep breath—it's not as hard as it seems!

The first thing to do, if you haven't done it already, is review the employee's performance file (see page 30) to remind yourself of key points about the employee's accomplishments during the year. Doing this should make you feel pretty confident about filling in the appraisal form. But if it doesn't, don't worry. Here are some ways to get beyond common new-manager anxieties about the writing stage:

"I'm not a good writer!" It's not essential for you to be a great writer to complete an appraisal—it's more important to be a great observer and recorder. And keep in mind the overall purpose of the performance appraisal form: to provide specific feedback on how your employees performed relative to their goals. That doesn't require any special magic, nor does it require riveting prose. What it does require is the ability to observe what happens and to accurately record it using clear language—brief phrases might be enough. It's even OK to use bullet points—just make it understandable, and keep it simple.

"I don't have enough information." Another common concern is that you don't have enough information to evaluate an employee. First of all, relax—you probably have more information than you think, or at least as much information as you need. Go back and look at the employee's performance log. If you still don't think you have enough information, take a closer look at any other documents, memos, or feedback notes you took throughout the year. Then, if you still feel like you don't have all the info you need, step back and ask yourself why you have this impression. Is it because the blank spaces on the form seem to require a couple of paragraphs, whereas you are capable at most of a couple of sentences? If so, that may still be OK—it isn't necessary to provide a lot of information—just detailed and useful information. Better to be concise and accurate than long-winded and vague.

"I have too much information." A different concern—but one that can feel just as challenging—is that you just have too much material collected. You may be wondering how you can boil down all those details to a few lines on a sheet of paper. However, though this may feel like a burden, having too much information is less of a problem than an advantage. The decision you need to make is what information is most important. Ask yourself what information best represents the highlights of the employee's performance during the appraisal period, and what information is not as relevant, or represents a minor, one-time-only situation or behavior. Examine the performance notes to see if you can group related comments together into larger categories, and then condense the information.

Write to the point

One of the most important things you'll need to do at this stage is to evaluate how much progress employees have made toward performance goals. These were likely set at the start of the appraisal period, and are often covered in the first section of the appraisal form.

To help you write effectively about these goals, consider revisiting the SMART technique (see page 68). Writing SMART means using the following principles to guide your assessment:

Specific: Assess performance using specific language, and words that speak to actual accomplishments. Choose words that connote actual, observable behaviors that the employee demonstrated, rather than words that speak to attitude or general personality traits.

Measurable: At the beginning of the performance appraisal period you wrote goals so that results could be easily measured (see page 66). Now is the time to measure the employee's achievement against whatever standards you set forth. Be careful to base your assessments on facts, not emotion.

Action-Oriented: Just as you used strong, action-oriented verbs when you developed goals at the beginning of the performance measurement period, use equally strong language at the end to describe what the employee actually accomplished.

Realistic: The goals that you and your employee collaboratively set at the beginning of the performance measurement period were realistic back then, and you revisited them throughout the year to make sure that they were still realistic. So as far as the "R" in SMART is concerned, your work should be done! If not, see page 147.

Time-bound: You also set goals that were time-bound—and you should have also revisited progress toward those goals. Now is your opportunity to see if the stated time frames were met.

IF THE GOALPOSTS HAVE CHANGED

If you've reached the writing phase of the performance appraisal process and find that the goals set at the last appraisal are not relevant to the employee's actual performance, then one of two things might have happened:

Workplace conditions have changed

Workplace conditions or circumstances may have changed so much since the last performance appraisal or regular feedback session that goals that were realistic a few months ago are unrealistic now. (For example, an employee's goal may have been to develop a customer feedback form for the company Web site, but then he was given a different Web project that took up all of his time.) If this is the case, all is not lost. Before you write the first appraisal draft, explain to the employee that you know the goalposts have changed and that this goal is no longer realistic. Then collaboratively determine a different standard against which the employee's performance will be measured.

You and the employee were out of sync

As a new or transferred manager, you may not have fully understood or supported the goals that the employee set with the previous manager, so during the time that you managed and evaluated his or her performance, you may not have focused on the crucial details. Goals are always a joint effort between a manager and an employee, and without a guiding hand, your employee may have lost direction and missed his or her goals. In this case, make note of what happened in the evaluation, and do not rate the employee on any goals that were "lost in the shuffle" due to lack of feedback or direction. If you are a new manager, you can help prevent this from happening in the first place by meeting with employees when you start to determine if adjustments in goals are necessary.

Assigning individual ratings

Once you've written the final draft of the appraisal, the next step is to rate each goal, competency (if relevant), and **section** of the performance appraisal form. (A section of the performance appraisal form refers to a cluster of similar items, such as goals or competencies.) The rating should summarize the performance examples you've listed. In other words, never start with the rating—finish with the rating.

Rating means assigning a number or descriptive phrase to each section of the employee's appraisal form. Systems for doing this take two main forms: nonmathematical and mathematical (see pages 24–25 for details). This means you'll either be assigning a number on a scale (probably from 1 to 3 or from 1 to 5) or a descriptive phrase or word, such as "exceeds expectations" or "outstanding."

Every finished performance appraisal form is different, so there's no one right way to rate individual items. However, you may find it helpful to keep these principles in mind as you begin this part of the process:

Assess each goal, competency, and section separately. Don't allow your overall impression or feelings about an employee to impact how you assess that person in any one area. Maintain your focus—and remember that almost everyone has areas of performance that are strong and areas that need work.

Base your rating for each section on the specifics that you have documented in that section. Avoid general details about performance; your goal here is to base your rating on specific examples.

Rate employees against the requirements of their specific jobs, not against each other. This is really the golden rule of doing performance appraisals.

Remember, your job isn't to "give" employees ratings. Your job is to accurately evaluate, assess, and identify the rating that an employee has already earned. To that end, avoid falling prey to rater errors, biases, or a "dartboard" approach to assigning ratings—and you'll do just fine.

FIRST PERSON INSIGHTS
Thinking outside the box

"Assigning ratings was always the hardest part of the form for me to complete! My company uses a simple 1 to 5 scale, so it's not that I had to do any complicated calculations. What was hard for me was feeling like I had to boil down each employee's performance into nondescript numbers. But while I still had to come up with those numbers, I stopped focusing on that so much and paid more attention to what those numbers really represent—which is a certain quality of performance, not a grade. Once I got myself thinking that way, I got my employees to think that way too. This really helped us all keep the whole rating thing in perspective."

Martyna W., Mahwah, NJ

The final rating

The last step in completing the appraisal form is usually assigning an overall rating to the employee's performance. This can be a nerve-wracking part of the process, but all you need to remember is that this rating is usually nothing more than an average (or a weighted average, depending on the form) of the ratings earned on all other sections of the form.

Naturally, employees tend to focus a lot on the final rating they are given—often more than on descriptions of their performance and ratings for individual goals—so you don't want to be hasty when assigning a number or phrase here.

Once you decide on a final rating, write it on your copy of the employee's final performance appraisal. This is the copy that you may then need to have approved by senior management or HR (see page 152). After it's approved, your organization may require you to give the employee an unsigned copy without the final rating for the employee to review (most HR experts recommend doing this about 30 to 45 minutes before the meeting; see page 154).

Wait to discuss the final rating with the employee in the meeting, when you will give him or her a completed, signed, approved copy of the appraisal with the final rating on it.

ASK THE EXPERTS

Why is it important not to communicate the overall rating until the performance appraisal meeting?

It's important to give the employee a copy of the appraisal without the overall rating (see page 154) so that the employee's focus stays on performance, rather than just on one number or label. Then, when you communicate the final rating during the meeting, stay attentive to the employee's reaction and do your best to refocus his or her attention back on performance.

DON'T WAIT TO RATE

Some managers prefer to wait until the appraisal meeting to assign a final rating, but this is not the best approach. It's always better to decide beforehand and write it on your copy of the appraisal form. One reason managers may wait until the last minute is that they want to be able to change the rating if they hear something unexpected during the meeting. If the employee has completed a self-appraisal form, however, the likelihood of this happening is slim. And despite the manager's intentions, the employee may wonder how much effort and objective assessment went into assigning the final rating if it's done on the spot at the meeting.

So what happens if you do assign a final rating, and then something unexpected comes up during the appraisal meeting that makes you wonder whether you evaluated the employee fairly? That's easy—you can always tell the employee that you need to reconsider the rating and get back to him or her. Being flexible and honest is the key here.

Obtaining approvals

You're almost there now! After you assign a final rating, all you need to do to consider the appraisal form completed and ready for the meeting is to obtain any necessary approvals.

The approvals required by organizations vary; some organizations don't require any other signatures besides the manager's. If you have this degree of autonomy, be particularly diligent to ensure that your appraisals are objective and accurate, since you won't have a second set of eyes looking at your work. You may want to consider going over it with your manager or with someone in HR, even if this is not officially required.

If you do need to get additional approvals, they may be from:

Your Manager Many organizations require that managers obtain approval from their own managers before performance appraisals are delivered to employees. While it may feel like extra work, there are some great benefits to this approach. For one thing, it's a great way to make sure that another set of eyes has reviewed every appraisal. After all, it is possible that, despite your best efforts to be objective, some rater error or bias may have crept into your appraisal. And it's a lot better for your manager to spot this—and help you correct it—than for your employee to find the problem.

Another benefit of obtaining next-level managerial approval is that it's a great way for your manager to get to know your direct reports better. This can help the whole organization function more efficiently—not to mention make it a friendlier place to work.

The Human Resources Department Some organizations require their HR department or director to review all completed performance appraisal forms before they are delivered to employees. This is especially true if a promotion or raise is tied to the review.

Once again, this may feel a bit frustrating at first, but there are valid reasons for taking this approach, too. First of all, HR experts sometimes have extensive experience with writing performance appraisals and may be able to offer valid suggestions on how to make your appraisals even stronger. Additionally, if performance ratings are tied to merit increases, HR may be able to identify whether enough money has been budgeted to cover the raises. HR staff may also be trained in identifying rater errors (see chapter 6)—especially ones occurring on an organization-wide scale, and help train managers to avoid bigger problems later on.

Giving employees a copy

When to let employees review the final appraisal

After the appraisal is approved, your organization may require you to give the employee an unsigned copy that does not have the final rating on it. Check with HR beforehand. When to give out the copy varies widely by organization. Here's a look at various approaches:

One or more days in advance

Pro: Giving employees a copy several days in advance provides ample time to read, review, and develop questions about the appraisals.

Cons: This approach increases the likelihood that if employees respond to the appraisal negatively, they can become somewhat fixed in that perception. This is because they'll have several days to form an opinion and to show their appraisal to other people who may reinforce that opinion. By the time the meeting takes place, they may be less interested in discussing it openly than in telling you about their impressions of how you appraised them.

30 to 45 minutes before the performance appraisal meeting

Pros: Giving employees 30 to 45 minutes before the meeting to review their copy affords them enough time to read the appraisal privately and to write down a few questions—both of which are important activities for employees to be able to do privately. Another advantage is that this is probably not long enough for employees to form rigid opinions about what you have written, or to tell others about how you evaluated them. This time frame allows employees enough time to process what you've written, but not enough time to script a fixed response.

Cons: Some employees like to have a night to "sleep on it," or really dissect what you have written and draft a response. They might also like to have time to compare notes with others before they go in to speak with you, or to see what their friends or family members think. Employees who have had a longer time for this process at other jobs may initially balk at having only 30 to 45 minutes.

At the start of the performance appraisal meeting

Pros: Managers who don't give their employees a copy of the appraisal until the start of the meeting can be absolutely certain that employees won't be unduly influenced by the opinions of coworkers, friends, or relatives ahead of time. Additionally, they will get employees' first reactions—which some managers believe are employees' most honest reactions. These managers think this allows them to work with employees on the basis of how the employee really feels, rather than on the image the employee presents.

Cons: Employees' first reactions to a performance appraisal are not always their lasting reactions. Employees may prefer the opportunity to have a private, unwitnessed reaction to their first reading of the performance appraisal and to formulate well-thought-out questions in advance.

ASK THE EXPERTS

Why do I need to give my employee an unsigned copy of the appraisal before the meeting, instead of just an official, signed copy?

Giving an unsigned copy is important because the appraisal process isn't truly complete until you've reviewed the appraisal with the employee and he or she has signed the original document. Once you have the employee's signature, you can give the employee a copy of the form that includes all of the required signatures and the final rating. Always be sure to check with your HR department before you give out copies of any kind to the employee.

Helpful resources

Tools you can use

BOOKS

How to Do a Superior Performance Appraisal
by William S. Swan

The #1 Guide to Performance Appraisals: Doing It Right!
by James E. Neal, Jr.

10 Minute Guide to Performance Appraisals
by Dale Furtwengler

WEB SITES

Handbook for Measuring Employee Performance
www.opm.gov/perform/wppdf/ 2002/handbook.pdf
A complete resource manual for managers.

Zigon Performance Group
www.zigonperf.com
From the home page of this site, you can subscribe to a free bimonthly performance measurement newsletter.

CHAPTER TEN

THE APPRAISAL MEETING

Setting the stage

Put some thought into where to hold the meeting

Where a meeting takes place can have a major impact on its outcome. A noisy, cluttered, cramped space can signal a lack of concern for the well-being of the participants. For that reason, important meetings are usually held in rooms designed to facilitate meetings. These rooms are quiet, comfortable, and well lit. Does a performance appraisal meeting qualify as a important meeting? Yes. Think about it. At this meeting you will be reviewing the work of a direct report for the entire year. While it may not seem a big deal to you, it most definitely will be a big deal to your employees. For this reason, it's better not to hold the meeting in your office or theirs, if possible. A conference room is usually the best setting for a performance appraisal discussion because it is neutral territory, and you're probably less likely to be interrupted. Also, conference rooms usually contain fewer distracting items than personal offices (photos, knickknacks, etc.), which can break the concentration of you and your employees.

Table Style: If you have a choice of various conference rooms, chose one with a round table. A round table allows you to sit to the side of the employee. This helps to create an setting that is nonconfrontational and nonthreatening. If it's a rectangular or square table, try to position yourself close to the employee, but not too close. Sitting "kitty corner"—with the employee at one end of the table and you on the side—is a good way to show support while still respecting employees' personal space. If it's a very small table, though, you might want to sit across from the employee, because not having enough of a barrier can hamper effective communication, too.

USING YOUR OFFICE

Sometimes you have no choice but to use your office for a performance appraisal meeting. (Your company may not have conference rooms, or if they do, they may be in use.) If you are using your office, here are some ways to minimize distractions and make this meeting (and any others, for that matter) more effective.

Desks: Avoid sitting across the desk from your employee. The desk represents your authority, and it can also create a substantial physical (and psychological) barrier between you and the person. Consider sitting at a table, if you have one in your office, or placing two chairs across from each other on the same side of the desk. Also, make sure the employee's chair is the same height as yours. If your chair is higher, it may seem like you're looking down at the employee—which is definitely not the message you want to send. If your chair is lower, the employee could unintentionally get the message that he or she is in control of the meeting, not you.

Computers: Keeping your computer on during the meeting is fine as long as you don't look at it, it doesn't make any noise when new e-mail comes in, and the employee can't see your monitor. So turn down the volume, and, if necessary, turn off your monitor.

Phones/Pagers/Cell Phones: A ringing telephone can be a real distraction, even if you don't answer it. It interrupts conversation and breaks the train of thought. If your phone has a feature that allows you to forward calls automatically to voice mail, use it. Otherwise, consider silencing the ringer, or unplugging the handset. If you like to keep these devices on in meetings in case you need to be reached in an emergency, ask yourself this: How often do emergencies occur? For most of us, it's not very often. Instead of keeping these devices on, or even setting them to vibrate, schedule ample time between appraisal meetings to check your voice mail and e-mail and respond to any urgent messages that might have come in.

Scheduling the time

The average performance appraisal meeting takes about 45 to 60 minutes, or up to 90 minutes for reviews of more senior management. During this time, you need to cover all the points in the appraisal, as well as have time to answer your employee's questions. Because these are such important meetings to your direct reports, is best to schedule it at optimum times.

It's generally not a good idea to conduct performance appraisal meetings in the early morning or late afternoon. It's also not a good idea to schedule them right before or after particularly busy times of the day. If you do, there's the possibility that either the performance meeting—or the busy time—could run late and throw off your schedule. When it comes to the performance appraisal meeting, managing your time well is a key factor.

It is also vital that you stick to the date and time you agreed upon. Canceling the meeting for anything other than an emergency sends a signal that this meeting is not very important.

Schedule your time in the meeting. At the beginning, set out the agenda—then stick to it. Allot enough time to cover each section of the appraisal form thoroughly and equally, and schedule in time at the end for discussing the final rating and any issues that my be brought up during the meeting.

MEETING HANDOUTS

Have these papers ready before your meeting:

■ An outline of the meeting. Type or write out a general outline of what you plan to cover and in what order, and review this with the employee when the meeting starts. This outline will help you both keep on track and avoid falling into unrelated conversations.

■ Copies of your final draft of the appraisal and of the employee's self-appraisal.

■ If there are major discrepancies between those two forms that you want to discuss, bring in any documents that pertain to this. That way, if there is any disagreement, you'll be able to show the employee exactly what you are referring to.

The meeting: step by step

Handling the beginning, middle, and end of the appraisal meeting

So it's finally time to hold the performance appraisal meeting. What's the first thing you should do? Relax—and help your employee to relax, too. Then work your way through these steps:

Step 1: Even though you are already well acquainted with your direct report, take a moment or two to build rapport by asking how his day is going or just offering him a glass of water.

Step 2: Go over your outline and give him an idea of what you'll be discussing.

Step 3: Give a brief overview of performance and relate the final rating (see page 150). Hand the final copy to the employee and give him a moment or two to look over it, then to comment on the final rating.

Step 4: Work your way through the appraisal section by section. This will help you avoid sandwiching bad news (see page 200). Stay in control of the meeting; as the manager giving the appraisal, you will probably need to do the majority of the talking and ask directed questions to elicit comments.

Step 5: Allow the employee to comment or ask questions about each section or point you make. If you had to reconcile any discrepancies between his self-appraisal and your final one, explain how you did this and show documentation if necessary (see page 116). If you hear anything new, jot down a few notes. Your employees may also want to take notes, and if so, encourage it!

Step 6: Be sure to ask the employee whether he has anything else he'd like to add; there may be something that didn't fit neatly into one of the categories.

Step 7: Set a date and time for a meeting to set future goals, to discuss the employee's increase, and/or to follow up on action plan development.

Step 8: Thank the employee and try to end on a positive, upbeat note.

ASK THE EXPERTS

How do I keep the meeting to its scheduled time?

Don't keep glancing at your watch. This sends a signal of impatience or boredom. Instead, position a clock right behind where you expect the employee to sit. Try to keep the clock around eye level so you can see it in your peripheral version or glance at it every once in a while without taking your attention away from the employee.

Last time I did appraisals, I had one employee who constantly interrupted me. What can I do this time around to prevent that?

The best thing you can do to keep this employee from interrupting is to speak to him about this as soon as he interrupts—which probably isn't something he does only during performance appraisal meetings. Before the meeting takes place, if he interrupts you while you are talking with him about something else, mention this behavior to him immediately and ask him to be more conscious of it. As with any other behavior that gets in the way of performance, be sure to address it up front, following the guidelines that are in place for providing constructive feedback (see page 206).

If it happens again during the meeting, emphasize how his interruptions keep you from conducting and delivering a fair and thorough appraisal, which hurts both of you. If he says he feels he will forget what he wants to say if he cannot interject when you're talking, ask him to jot down notes instead, then give him a chance to speak when you're done.

Body language

Pay attention to what goes unsaid

The first five minutes of an appraisal meeting can easily set the tone for the rest. As you go about breaking the ice with your employee, perhaps by asking how his day is going so far, start paying attention to his body language.

Why? Simply put, you can learn a lot from an employee's body language about how he is reacting to your performance feedback. Is he relaxed, yet attentive? Making eye contact? Smiling when appropriate? How is he sitting? An employee who is slumped in his seat during the meeting could be upset with what he is hearing or not overly concerned about helping the meeting run well. If the employee sits with his arms folded tightly across his chest or in a hunched, defensive position, this might seem to contradict his statement that he's "been very good with customer service this year." (Of course, you must be careful not to assume that body language has one specific meaning; that same person who crossed his arms may just be cold. So pay attention to the entire environment and context before jumping to any conclusions.)

Be aware of your own body language as well. Fiddling with things on your desk, tapping your fingers, looking out the window repeatedly, and checking your watch are all signs of impatience and disinterest. Be an active listener, keeping your posture relaxed and approachable and keeping an open expression on your face. Don't interrupt and don't let silences drag on for too long. Be friendly and direct as you work your way through the employee's appraisal form.

NONVERBAL CLUES:
WHAT EMPLOYEES REALLY THINK

What your employees say to you during the meeting is important, but so is what they don't say to you. Be sensitive to any nonverbal messages. As you interact with your employees during the performance appraisal process, pay attention to:

Eye contact: Is an employee who usually maintains good eye contact with you suddenly finding it difficult to look directly at you?

Body movements: Has an employee begun to unconsciously move his or her hands or feet, or fidget with jewelry, pens, or other objects? Is the employee suddenly crossing his or her arms or legs, or pulling his or her body or head away slightly?

Speech: Is an employee suddenly speaking haltingly, in a different tone of voice, or at a different rate?

None of these nonverbal indicators, by themselves, necessarily means that the employee is uncomfortable. What you should be looking for is patterns, and if you see a change in the pattern, this could indicate that you've touched on a sensitive area that you'll want to explore further. In this case, encourage the employee to talk with you about that particular topic in more depth.

Communicating ratings

In appraisal meetings where the final rating is delivered at the end, it can be all too easy for employees to fixate on what that rating will be. They may spend the meeting engaging in mental arithmetic, trying to figure out how all of the individual and section ratings "add up." And you might be distracted, too—especially if you're anxious about how the employee might react to the rating.

The best way to get around this is to give the overall rating at the beginning of the appraisal meeting, especially if the employee is not going to be pleased with the rating. This is the best way to get the news out on the table and begin dealing with it constructively.

How you communicate the rating is just as important as when you do it. Think of yourself as a reporter in this situation: Your role is not to judge, but to be honest, objective, and thorough in your evaluation of employees' performance. It might help to use BASIC feedback principles (see page 196) to help you stick to the facts. Your report should be a summary of specific behaviors that lead you to your overall assessment. This is not a time to introduce new material.

To help you avoid passing judgment, realize that you are not "giving" the employee a final rating—you are merely communicating the rating that the employee already earned. When discussing the rating, choose language that empowers employees, rather than makes them feel they're on trial. Always give examples of behavior, rather than discussing your take on the employee's attitude. Stay away from negative statements like, "I'm giving you this final rating because I am not happy that you've been such a poor team player this year." Instead, take a more constructive and positive approach, such as, "Although your performance when it comes to teamwork can be improved, your performance met expectations in most other areas, earning you a final rating of . . . " This shifts the focus onto the behavior that earned the employee his or her final rating.

"I only worked for one manager before I joined another company as a supervisor a few years ago. He had been a pretty good manager, so I generally tried to follow his example. In performance appraisal meetings, he waited until the end to give the final rating, so that's how I did it, too. But I found this really didn't work well at my new company. Some employees would be badly surprised when, after a long talk about their achievements, they received a low or middling rating. One employee in particular, Ben, got very upset and walked out of the meeting. When I talked to him about it the next day, it was as if he had forgotten all of the positive things and only wanted to concentrate on his rating. I talked to another manager about this, and she told me she had taken a workshop where they suggested telling employees their rating at the beginning of the appraisal meeting instead. I was a little nervous about trying this, particularly when it came to Ben, because although he did better during the next appraisal period, he still wasn't fully meeting expectations. But at his next appraisal, I mentioned his final rating right up front, and it turned out we were able to talk about it a lot more calmly. I think he finally understood why his rating was accurate, and we were then able to strategize about how he could earn a better rating the next time—which, by the way, he did!"

Tierney R., Stafford, VA

Topics to avoid

Things to steer clear of during the performance appraisal meeting

During the performance appraisal meeting, it can be easy for both you and the employee to get off track and onto topics that are not appropriate for this setting.

In particular, it may be tempting to give advice or share your own personal "war stories." But the conversation needs to remain on the employee and the employee's performance—not on you. While there is a time and a place for sharing your experiences, do not allow the focus of the meeting to shift from the employee to you. Be equally careful not to offer to solve employees' problems for them. Your intentions might be good, but doing this may actually disempower them and may even make those employees too dependent on you.

There are several other areas you should both be careful to avoid during the meeting. If your employee brings up the following topics, be diligent about getting the conversation back on track:

Other Employees Some employees may ask, "How does my evaluation compare to everyone else's?" You may be tempted to give the employee some sense of where he or she stands, but discussing other employees during an appraisal meeting is never a good idea because it can lead to unfair comparisons. If this topic comes up, focus the conversation back on the employee's performance and away from the performance of others.

Personal Issues Another employee might say, "You know I've been having some personal problems. I'm surprised that you can't cut me some slack." It's vital not to let performance appraisal discussions stray into personal issues—even if they are common knowledge. These sorts of issues can cloud discussions about performance, and can lead the employee to make excuses for why performance standards weren't met. However, if personal topics come up that are related to the work environment (for example, a possible instance of harassment or discrimination), let the employee know that you will take this up with HR, and then do so.

Money During the appraisal meeting, it's typical for employees to ask, "So what does this rating translate into in terms of a raise?" In most organizations, the merit increase discussion takes place separately from the performance appraisal meeting. If this is the case in your organization, don't be tempted to release this information now, even if you have it. Performance appraisal meetings should focus on performance—not on money. So keep the conversation focused on the appraisal, not on the raise. In this situation, tell the employee, "The purpose of this meeting is really to discuss your performance. I'd be happy to discuss salary with you at a separate meeting. So, back to the appraisal . . . ."

Managers can also find themselves getting into topics that should be avoided during the appraisals meeting. Some to be aware of include:

Confidential Information It's important not to allow your conversations with employees to stray into topics that are confidential, such as certain financial details or employee gossip. This can easily happen—even to managers who normally wouldn't think of sharing such information—especially if real rapport already exists, or develops between the manager and the employee during the meeting. Resist the urge, and don't forget that when you're a manager, there's no such thing as an "off the record" conversation.

Psychoanalysis You may have some theories about why a direct report is performing a certain way, which might be based on, say, your knowledge of the employee's family dynamics. However, it's not your role to play therapist during this meeting. Focus on workplace behaviors and on helping the employee develop solutions to workplace performance issues. If you have any theories, make sure they don't impact how you manage or assess your employees.

Career growth

Should you discuss where the employee can go from here?

Many managers wonder whether it's a good idea to discuss the employee's career trajectory within the organization during the appraisal meeting. While there is no one right approach, generally speaking, there are some good reasons for not discussing a possible promotion or far-distant raise at this point. Concerns include:

Past vs. Future The performance appraisal is essentially a review of employees' performance over the past year. It is not about their future, but about what has happened already. In general, it is best to save those future-oriented discussions for the meeting when you and your employee set future goals.

Being Fair If you discuss potential with some employees—such as your top performers—it's only fair to discuss it with all of them. But the reality is that not all employees have the potential to eventually advance to positions of greater responsibility within the organization. This may not be bad news for those who are truly happy to keep on performing solidly in their current positions. Others, however, may find this news devastating. In those situations, the purpose—and value—of the performance appraisal can be lost amidst the realization that a long-desired promotion probably will never materialize.

Perceived Promises A final problem with discussing potential is that if you tell the employee that he or she has the potential to advance within the organization at a later date, that employee's hopes will become fixed on the promotional opportunity. But suppose this employee's performance deteriorates sometime after that statement is made, and he or she is no longer in line for the promotion. Or suppose the employee is found not to possess all of the skills required for the position, and someone else is selected. Or suppose there is a change in business conditions and the promotional opportunity is no longer available. Imagine how disappointed the employee would feel in these scenarios. Trying to prevent this by telling an employee ahead of time that "a discussion of potential does not constitute a promise" isn't likely to help either—if the promotion does not come through, the employee may still feel cheated, and could easily get disgruntled and move on.

Problems that can arise

Appraisal meetings come in many different flavors

No matter how carefully you prepare before conducting performance appraisals, things may not always go according to plan. Some problems to be on the lookout for:

Apathy

What it looks like: It's possible that an employee could choose to simply disengage himself emotionally during the performance appraisal meeting, especially if he doesn't like what he's hearing. In this case, you might notice monotone, brief answers, long pauses, speaking with averted eyes, and other signs of distraction.

What to do about it: Describe to the employee, in a nonthreatening way, what you are observing, and encourage the employee to talk with you about what's on his mind. It's best not to demand that the employee tell you what he's feeling—for instance, by asking, "Why don't you care about this?" or "Why isn't this important to you?" Instead, offer objective, behavior-based observations. ("You're only giving very brief responses. That's unusual for you. Is there something on your mind or some other issue you'd like to discuss?") Then give the employee an opportunity to explain.

Strong Emotion

What it looks like: This can take many forms: anger (yelling), sadness (tears), frustration (balled fists or bulging eyes), and so on.

What to do about it: If the employee is reacting with tears, give her a tissue—and perhaps a few minutes to collect herself. If the employee is reacting in anger, allow her to react, then redirect the conversation back to the topic of her performance. If appropriate, reassure the employee afterward that many people react emotionally during performance appraisal discussions.

Conflict

What it looks like: Conflict is a lot like anger, but it may be a bit more confrontational—and that confrontation may be aimed directly at you. The employee may level accusations or play "the blame game."

What to do about it: Above all, don't allow yourself to become angry. Matching one confrontational reaction with an equally confrontational one will only intensify the conflict and make it more difficult to get back to the topic of the employee's performance.

In all three of these cases, it's important to realize that there may come a time when you need to make a judgment call; specifically, should you continue the performance appraisal meeting or reschedule it? If you do decide it's not possible to complete the meeting, reschedule it before the end the first meeting, preferably for the next day. At the beginning of the next meeting, be willing to clear the air, let go of what happened in the first meeting, and then move forward productively.

ASK THE EXPERTS

What if the employee just sits there silently and won't participate in the performance appraisal discussion?

Find out what's going on. Give the employee feedback on what you are observing—and keep that feedback behavioral. Instead of saying, "Obviously you aren't taking this process—or your own performance—seriously, since you're just sitting there," first explain to the employee why participation in this meeting will benefit both of you. Then, try to encourage the employee to speak with you about any concerns he or she might have about the process. Be sure to explain that if you don't know what the concerns are, you won't be able to address them and help the employee get past them.

Closing and following up

It's not the end . . . it's just the beginning

Once you've reached the end of the performance appraisal discussion, what comes next? This is the time to talk next steps with your employee, being careful not to make any promises for the future that might be unrealistic (see page 171).

In some organizations, this is when you set a time to meet with the employee and discuss a merit increase. In other companies, the next step might be arranging a meeting to set goals for the new appraisal period (see Chapter 4), or to discuss the employee's development plan (see Chapter 5), if that talk didn't take place during the performance appraisal meeting. Always set a specific date and time when you and the employee will meet again (yes—open your calendar and make an appointment!)—and do this before you end the meeting.

Generally speaking, both the raise meeting and the goal-setting meeting are held separately from the appraisal meeting. This is partly to ensure that the appraisal meeting is etched into the employee's mind as purely a discussion about past performance. Setting upcoming meetings to plan for the future also helps to make the performance appraisal cycle an ongoing and vibrant process.

Planning a time to talk about future goals reminds the employee that there is hope—and another chance right around the corner to improve performance. Reinforcing this sense of hope in a realistic and honest manner is key to keeping employees motivated. It promotes the idea of a "new beginning" in which the slate of last year's performance is wiped clean and anything is possible.

So, in closing the meeting, show your commitment to this new beginning by setting the dates for taking these next steps with the employee. Then, don't let your work commitments force you to push these dates back. Stay on top of the process now, and it will be that much easier to wrap things up at the end of the next performance appraisal period.

ASK THE EXPERTS

Besides setting a time to set new goals, what kind of follow-up do I need to do after the performance appraisal meeting?

For one thing, follow up on any unfinished business that came up during the meeting. This could mean looking into a complaint the employee had about a particular procedure or reviewing more closely the employee's workload to try to help him or her manage it better—any number of things.

It may also mean checking in with the employee a few weeks after the meeting to see how he or she is coming along with any action plan that you worked out collaboratively during the meeting to improve any areas of performance that do not meet standards, or it may mean following up on certain parts of the employee's development plan. As always, take notes on any follow-up you do, and make sure the employee does the same.

Helpful resources

Tools you can use

BOOKS

How to Improve Performance Through Appraisal and Coaching by Donald L. Kirkpatrick

Productive Performance Appraisals (Worksmart Series) by Randi Toler Sachs

Info-line: How to Conduct a Performance Appraisal by Steve Hickman

WEB SITES

U.S. Coast Guard
www.uscg.mil/leadership/ news/fall99/conduct.htm
"Conducting Good Performance Appraisal Meetings," written for U.S. Coast Guard managers but relevant to many types of managers, provides a step-by-step approach to the appraisal meeting.

"Make Performance Appraisal Relevant"
www.unep.org/restrict/pas/paspa. htm
This in-depth article by management professor Winston Oberg discusses how to make performance appraisals more relevant to organizations.

CHAPTER ELEVEN

PROGRESSIVE DISCIPLINE

Know the warning signs

If an employee is clearly having problems, offer help—but carefully

For some reason, one of your employees seems to be settling into some bad habits. You overlook it a few times, but the poor performance continues. Your anxiety level rises. What is going on? When should you intervene? Do you need to note these problems on his next performance appraisal? What are you supposed to do now?

First things first—don't get frantic. There are five main reasons a employee might not be meeting your expectations (see page 179), and many of them can be corrected easily and do not require documentation in a performance appraisal.

The first thing to do in the case of an underperforming employee is to call him in for a talk about his performance. Do this as soon as you notice a pattern developing. Put your employee at ease by establishing rapport first, perhaps by asking what the employee is working on that day. Then move into describing and discussing the situation, using the BASIC guidelines for corrective feedback (see page 196).

As you explain the problem, be clear and succinct. Don't beat around the bush and don't try to soften the blow by using qualifying words and phrases such as "maybe you could work a little faster" or "you might want to try to come to Monday morning meetings on time."

Ask the employee to share his perspective on the situation and to outline a workable solution and a time frame for it, but don't try to solve the employee's performance problem for him. You're there to support, not to "save" him. Let him know you're interested in how he plans to improve his performance and find out how he feels about the work he's doing now, because the problem might lie there (such as too much or not enough work). Always get his take on the feedback you've given before you end the meeting. Don't end the discussion until you're sure he understands exactly what is expected of him and can articulate it.

POSSIBLE REASONS FOR
EMPLOYEES' POOR PERFORMANCE

■ **They still don't know how to do the job.** You may have felt your training or tutorial was enough for the employee to learn the ropes, but he still isn't clear on what to do. Other people you've hired may have picked up on certain aspects of the position faster, but remember that each employee is different and will have varied strengths. If more training will do the trick, the fix is easy. If not, then you will need to take stronger action (see page 182).

■ **They thought they were doing the job.** This is one of the reasons why early feedback is so critical. Many managers are reluctant to criticize employees and they fail to correct mistakes, especially when employees are learning new skills. Absent that feedback, the employee thinks he's doing a fine job—only to find out later he was underperforming.

■ **They misunderstood the job priorities.** It's possible that the employee would be doing the job you wanted her to do, but she misunderstood what you wanted her to focus her energies on. If she is spending an inordinate amount of time on a low-priority task, then you can easily correct the problem with a little communication and clarification.

■ **They have conflicting tasks.** In cases where an employee is reporting to or receiving instruction from more than one manager, he may be unable to complete tasks to anyone's satisfaction, and may be reluctant to come forward with the problem. Once you confirm this with him, discuss the problem with the other manager to find an appropriate solution.

■ **They have a personal problem.** If a new employee is spending a lot of work time on personal calls or coming in late, she may be coping with difficulties at home. If you know this is the case, there may be things you can do to help (see page 181 on Employee Assistance Programs).

Personal problems

Get feedback and set the stage for improvement

If you suspect that an employee has a personal problem, you may feel uncomfortable asking about it. That's only natural—no one likes to pry. And that's a good instinct to have, because in fact you need to be careful about what you ask employees when it comes to personal problems. Legally, you cannot ask employees about their marital situation, criminal record, or any past drug or alcohol problems. If you suspect a current abuse problem or health issue, talk to HR before doing anything else; certain kinds of disabilities and conditions are protected by the Americans with Disabilities Act (ADA).

Whatever you suspect the problem is, to cover your legal bases, you must remain focused on his or her performance when dealing with this issue; it is not your role to determine if, in fact, the employee does have a substance abuse problem or is having a family crisis. You can, however, ask the employee to come and talk to you about how his or her performance is slipping. Be as respectful as you can, but be firm. Go over your list of concerns, citing specific behaviors.

A tactful (and legal) way to approach these issues could be saying something along the lines of, "Jack, I've noticed that you have been coming into work late these last two weeks and that the contract you were working on is still not done. What are your thoughts on this, and is there some way I can support you in getting your job done?"

Always follow the guidelines for a constructive feedback session (see page 206-207), no matter what you think the real issue is. Ask how you can help remedy the situation, keeping the focus on behavior and not on personality. This may also be a good time to remind the employee about your Employee Assistance Program, if you have one (see page 181). As always, formally document your concerns (see page 184). And in all cases, know which situations are protected by law, avoid inquiring directly about them, and respect the employee's right to privacy.

ASK THE EXPERTS

Are there some behaviors that should result in immediate dismissal, without warning or corrective measures?

Usually, yes. Your company should have a list of those unacceptable behaviors, which may also have legal ramifications. These behaviors could include:

- acting violently or threatening to act violently, including any fighting on the premises
- theft or destruction of company property
- downloading pornography
- record falsification or alteration
- using drugs or alcohol on the premises, or coming to work under the influence (includes failure of any mandatory drug test)
- unauthorized possession of weapons on the premises
- sexual harassment or assault

EAP: A RESOURCE FOR ALL EMPLOYEES

If your employee is having a personal problem, your company may have a program in place that can help: the Employee Assistance Program (EAP). This is designed to help employees with personal issues related to health, family, financial, marital, legal, and alcohol/drug problems, among others. An estimated 70% of Fortune 500 companies have an EAP. If your organization does offer this as a benefit, the employee's orientation kit will have information about it, but don't assume the employee knows about it. Let him know that EAP is there for just these kinds of problems—whatever they are—and encourage him to use the service. Stress that the counseling is strictly confidential.

Your discipline system

Managing people is one of the hardest jobs in corporate America. And it becomes a gut-wrenching job when you have to discipline employees who are not performing well. Fortunately, there is a management tool to help you with this dilemma. It is called **progressive discipline**. Progressive discipline refers to the series of formal steps that managers take to address performance concerns. These steps vary by organization, but may include verbal warnings, written warnings, perhaps suspension, and then termination. Large corporations usually have a company policy that you can reference. Either way, speak with your manager or someone in HR to help you become familiar with how it works.

Progressive discipline has three main functions:

- It formally communicates to the employee the need to improve performance. The much-hoped-for outcome is that the employee's performance turns around as a result.
- It provides formal steps to take if performance does not improve.
- It lays down a foundation for fairly terminating the employee while protecting the organization from wrongful discharge lawsuits.

The steps of progressive discipline are usually some combination of the following:

- **Initial warning** This is usually an informal meeting to address the problem and requires no formal write-up. If the behavior does not change, then the manager needs to start documenting it formally.

- **Second warning** This should be delivered both verbally and via written memo. The memo should detail the behavior or performance that still needs improvement, and may include a time frame. (If you set a time frame, however, be careful that you don't unintentionally imply that the employee is guaranteed employment through that date, regardless of performance. Get help from your HR department or legal counsel to develop language that helps you avoid this potential legal pitfall.) At this stage, a concrete plan for performance improvement should be devised, and the standards clarified.

- **Suspension** Requiring a paid or unpaid leave from the job may be the next step, especially pending investigation into a performance problem.

- **Termination** The final resort, when all other measures have failed, is to end the employment relationship.

ASK THE EXPERTS

I had to give an employee a verbal warning about his poor performance six months ago. He fixed the problem and all is well. Do I need to document this in his upcoming performance appraisal?

Performance appraisals should reflect the employee's performance during the entire performance measurement period. By documenting the poor performance and how the employee corrected it, you are being fair to him—and to all of your other employees as well. You're also showing that the employee addressed and corrected a performance issue, which can reflect well on both of you.

How long do I have to use progressive discipline before I can terminate?

Most companies use windows of 30, 60, or 90 days. As a manager, you need to consider what negative impact the poor performance is having and decide based on that; i.e., don't let it slide 90 days if sales are being affected or if service is slipping within the first 30.

Documenting fairly

Keep it SMART, keep it legal

As you integrate the performance appraisal system into your ongoing management practices, always stay current with practices that are looked on favorably from a legal perspective. In this spirit, stick close to the following principles as you manage your employees year-round:

Ensure that your assessments and appraisals of employees remain bias-free

Don't allow factors unrelated to performance to enter into your assessments. In addition to being familiar with common appraisal errors (see chapter 6), this means not allowing any factors that are protected by federal, state, or local laws to enter into your management or record-keeping practices. On a federal level, protected status includes such things as gender, race, color, age, religion, pregnancy, national origin, and disability. On a state or local level, this could include things like sexual orientation, marital status, or political affiliation.

Maintain consistent documentation on all of your employees

This means keeping the same kind of objective, bias-free records on everyone. Otherwise, you could be accused of targeting an employee or group of employees for less favorable treatment because of some characteristic. If that characteristic happens to be something that is protected by federal, state, or local law, such "selective documentation" might be perceived as discriminatory.

Communicate performance expectations to employees clearly and in advance

Make sure goals are SMART (see page 68) and that the behaviors on which you are basing your assessments are measurable and/or observable. Stay away from gut feelings and from subjective assessments of performance.

Document appropriately

Document actions and behaviors related to the job, not to personality or attitude. And maintain documentation on an ongoing basis—rather than trying to fill in the blanks right before you complete an employee's performance appraisal or before disciplining or terminating the employee. In your documentation, take a simple and direct approach. Ever heard of the "5 Ws and an H" technique? If you document "who, what, when, where, why (if you know why), and how," you should have most of the information you need.

Communicate to employees what the consequences will be if they don't bring their performance up to the expected level

These consequences should not come as a surprise. Then, follow through on those consequences consistently: Avoid making idle threats and carrying through on consequences only with certain employees.

Allow—and encourage—employees to ask questions and converse with you about their performance

In addition to being good management practice, this is also sound from a legal perspective. Managers who seem arbitrary or capricious are less likely to be judged positively if there is ever a challenge to a performance-related action. Remember—as long as your employees are still employed, there is still hope, and you must maintain a willingness to support, coach, guide, and direct them. Two-way conversation is a critical element of this.

Acting in good faith

Legal issues to consider

Having a well-documented case against an employee before taking disciplinary action is one of the best ways to avoid legal problems. Former employees can sue for wrongful termination if they can prove that their employer has breached what is known as an implied commitment to **good faith and fair dealing**. This is based on the notion that every employment relationship, regardless of whether an actual contract was signed, promises fair treatment.

In other words, if you fire an employee for seemingly arbitrary reasons, you could be headed for trouble. This may be more of a risk with a recently hired employee, since you haven't had the time to demonstrate any commitment to that person. (Again, document, document, document.)

One bad apple

"I had a salesperson who was probably the hardest-working person I ever had on my staff. She came in early, worked late, and was great when it came to customer service, but she couldn't sell a thing. Whenever a customer had an objection to a product, she wouldn't say a word. I tried training her and thought she was doing better only to learn that she was making up answers to customers' questions. I tried to give her the benefit of the doubt for as long as I could, but finally, after about six months, I started giving her verbal and written warnings and eventually had to let her go. It was rough—but what happened after I let her go was even rougher. Within two weeks, my best two salespeople quit. They both told me that they had started looking five months ago because they were tired of 'carrying' my hard-working nonseller. I was sorry to see these employees go, but it taught me a valuable lesson. I now understand the impact a poor performer can have on the entire workplace, and how important it is to start trying to help the employee correct that poor performance right from the very beginning."

Alex L., Fargo, ND

Termination

When there are no more chances left

It is one of the most difficult situations you will likely end up facing as a manager. What is it? Terminating an employee. Or, as some managers prefer to think of it, presiding over a situation in which an employee has terminated him- or herself due to poor performance.

What next? If termination is imminent, you need to review your company's termination policy and alert your HR department to make sure your legal bases are covered. Before the meeting, you may want to consider inviting another supervisor, usually an HR representative, to attend. In addition to providing the added comfort of having an extra person in the room, this witness will also be able to attest to the fairness of the meeting.

During the termination meeting, treat your employee in a dignified and respectful manner. Remember that the employee's inability or unwillingness to bring performance up to expected standards has nothing to do with his or her worth and value as a person. Explain in concise but specific language why the employee is being terminated. Make it clear that the decision is final and cannot be negotiated. Keep the conversation focused on performance—and keep it short.

If the employee is expected to leave immediately, be clear about how and when this should happen, and have the final check, severance or vacation compensation checks, and any other forms related to benefits ready ahead of time.

ASK THE EXPERTS

Should I offer severance pay?

If a severance arrangement was part of the initial negotiation with the employee, then you must honor that agreement. Barring any previous arrangements, adhere to your company's standard severance policy and do not deviate from it, lest you cause yourself problems with other departing employees later on. Generally speaking, companies do not offer severance in cases where the employee was on board for less than a year, but you should check with your HR department or legal counsel before you discuss this with the employee.

When is the best time to hold a termination meeting?

Some HR experts advocate doing it early in the day and early in the week, so that the employee isn't completely taken off guard after a full day or week of work. Others advise holding the meeting as late in the day as possible so that there are fewer employees around to witness the the employee pack up and exit, to spare the employee embarrassment, and to avoid disrupting the workday. Still, there is no one "right time" for this, and your decision should depend on how you anticipate both the terminated employee and other employees will handle the news.

Resignation

Treat this as a way to gain new insights into your organization

In some discipline cases, an employee will decide to resign before you can terminate him or her. This may happen because the employee is as dissatisfied with employment at your organization as you are with his or her performance, or because the employee is trying to bow out before being terminated (which will not look very promising to future employers). Or the employee may decide to resign because he or she has found a new job.

Whatever the reason, try to arrange an exit interview before this employee leaves. Like a job interview, the exit interview allows you to gain insight into the fit between an employee and your organization. In cases where an employee has resigned due to disagreement over his or her performance, such a discussion may reveal hidden issues about your organization or management style that you might use to prevent similar problems from cropping up in the future.

Exit interviews can be done either orally or via questionnaire. The latter defuses some of the awkwardness and may lead to greater honesty. On the other hand, without being able to assess body language or nonverbal cues (see page 164), it may be harder to know whether you're getting the truth.

Whichever method you use, ask questions (see page 191) to get to the heart of the matter. You may learn some surprising things that didn't come up during regular feedback sessions or the progressive discipline process. You may learn, for example, that the terminated employee did not receive enough training or direction, or you may learn that other employees somehow impeded this employee's performance. Of course, not all departing employees will leap at the chance to help the company that just let them go by explaining such things, but if you have treated this employee fairly through the termination process, he or she might be more willing to answer some questions that could help you with the next hire.

During the exit interview, listen with an open mind and take notes. And be careful not to let the exit interview turn into a blame session. If you sense that the discussion is veering that way, redirect the conversation or draw it to a close. The important point here is that you use this interview to bring closure to the relationship by allowing an employee to speak his or her mind, and that you use this knowledge to help you manage more effectively in the future.

10 GREAT EXIT INTERVIEW QUESTIONS

Here are some solid questions to include in the exit interview or questionnaire:

1. How do you feel you were treated here as an employee?
2. What do you think could have been done differently?
3. Under what circumstances might you have stayed on?
4. Did you feel you were given enough support in your job?
5. Did you feel you were given adequate training? Are there any other training opportunities that you think you should have been offered?
6. How do you feel your qualifications and skills could have been used to better advantage?
7. Was the job different than you imagined it would be? How?
8. Did you have any concerns that weren't handled appropriately?
9. Did you feel that there was enough cooperation in your department, or was there too much competition?
10. Are there any other issues you wish to raise?

Helpful resources

Tools you can use

BOOKS

101 Sample Write-Ups for Documenting Employee Performance Problems: A Guide to Progressive Discipline and Termination
by Paul Falcone

Dealing with Problem Employees: A Legal Guide
by Amy DelPo and Lisa Guerin

Toxic Emotions at Work: How Compassionate Managers Handle Pain and Conflict
by Peter J. Frost

From Hiring to Firing: The Legal Survival Guide For Employers
by Steven Mitchell Sack

WEB SITES

Mercer Human Resource Consulting
www.mercerhr.com/knowledge-center/reportsummary.jhtml/dynamic/idContent/1086910
Find out about the cost of implementing an employee assistance program.

HR Solutions
www.hrsolutionsinc.com/ov/overture_eia.htm
This management solutions company offers an Exit Interview Assessment.

Managing People: Problem Employees
www.businesstown.com/people/employees.asp
This section from BusinessTown.com offers employers a guide to different kinds of problem employees—and how to handle them.

Got Trouble
www.gottrouble.com/legal/business/severance_benefits.html
Tips on negotiating severance, specifically for small business managers.

CHAPTER TWELVE

FEEDBACK FOR ONGOING SUCCESS

The value of feedback

Giving feedback is critical to helping employees improve performance during the performance measurement period. Good managers provide feedback on a regular basis, such as at weekly staff meetings, during which a manager might say, "Jim, your presentation to the board convinced them to accept our proposal. Thanks for your great work on this." Good managers also take advantage of opportunities to give informal feedback on a daily basis, and strive to create an open climate in which employees feel comfortable asking for feedback at any time.

Because feedback is so important, some managers have a formal feedback meeting every three months, called a QPD (Quarterly Performance Discussion). At other companies, these meetings are held monthly or biannually. There is no one correct frequency for giving feedback; it depends on your company and your style as a manager.

Regular feedback meetings allow you to take stock of an employee's performance to date and are also good opportunities to:

Assess Goals Evaluate the progress your employees have made toward reaching the goals they set at the start of the new performance appraisal period. Discuss whether they need to be modified or deleted. If this is the case, collaboratively develop new goals that reflect the changes (see page 147).

Assess Competencies Determine how well employees are demonstrating the skills and competencies that have been identified as important for the position and the organization. Put new needs into an employee development plan (see chapter 5), then monitor their progress regularly.

Give Feedback Reinforce what employees have done well with positive feedback and coach them in how to continue performing well. You may need to give constructive or corrective feedback (see pages 206–209). Follow up at the next meeting to find out how the employee is addressing these performance issues.

ASK THE EXPERTS

My employees seem satisfied with their yearly appraisals. Won't monthly feedback sessions just add another time burden?

If employees are not given regular feedback from you about how well they are progressing toward their goals, it will be hard for them to know when they are getting off course, to say nothing of the time they will waste being off track. Explain to your employees that if you wait until the yearly appraisal meeting to tell employees that they did not meet their goals, this would be unfair to them because you would be holding back information they need to correct their course before it's too late.

THE BENEFITS OF REGULAR FEEDBACK

■ Feedback reinforces desired behaviors, which increases the likelihood that employees will continue behaving in these ways. Otherwise, employees may not fully realize that their actions are having a positive impact.

■ Feedback makes employees aware of nonproductive, counterproductive, or otherwise problematic behaviors. Without this information, employees may not realize that what they are doing is ineffective. With this information, employees can work on changing these behaviors.

■ Feedback provides a daily reminder to the employee that performance standards and measures are important to the organization, to you, and to them.

Keep feedback BASIC

Providing ongoing feedback is one of the best ways to promote communication between you and your employees—and that can only help you all do your jobs. Just be sure to let employees know ahead of time that you're going to be giving them performance feedback. Then keep it simple (and brief) by following these BASIC guidelines:

Behavior-Based: Feedback should relate to behavior, not to attitude or personality. Focus on employees' observable actions and talk to them about how these actions positively or negatively impact their performance and their goals. Employees will probably prefer talking about their behavior to talking about your perceptions of their attitude or personality, since they'll be less likely to feel as though you are judging or criticizing them.

ASAP—As Soon as Possible: Give employees feedback about their performance and behavior as soon as you can. Of course you would never want to embarrass an employee by offering constructive feedback in public, and not everyone is comfortable being praised in front of other people, either. So, find—or create—the first possible opportunity to give feedback in the right setting.

Specific: Be precise with the words you use to give feedback, and avoid any that might mean something different to you than to your employees. Give them enough info so that they understand exactly what they should keep doing, or what they need to do differently.

Interactive: Leave time during feedback sessions to let employees jump in with comments and ideas. They may have their own new and creative ideas about how to sustain or improve their performance.

Consistent: Ongoing feedback will help ensure that you and your employees have a consistent view of what is expected, as well as a consistent understanding of how well those expectations are being met.

A FEW MORE FEEDBACK GUIDELINES

Building on the idea that feedback should be BASIC, keep these three additional principles in mind when you provide any type of feedback to your employees:

■ **Tell employees in advance.** Take away the element of surprise by telling employees early and often that you are going to provide them with performance feedback. This is also the perfect time to tell them that you expect them to actively participate in the discussion, and gives them a chance to prepare.

■ **Address one topic at a time.** Whether you are praising, offering constructive criticism, or addressing more serious performance concerns, focus on one idea at a time. This can be a bit challenging at first, since many managers tend to think of employees in general terms as "good performers" or "poor performers," and then view all aspects of their performance within that framework. If you heed the "A" in BASIC, however, and give feedback as soon as possible, you'll find it easier to address each topic individually, as it comes up. This approach will also help you avoid overwhelming employees with concerns about their performance, or lavishing so much praise on them that they find it difficult to imagine how they could ever improve.

■ **Keep it brief.** While feedback needs to be interactive, there is no value in needlessly extending feedback discussions with employees. Get to the point—succinctly.

Types of feedback

Before you start giving feedback to an employee, make sure you know what kind of feedback you want to give. There are three main types:

- **Positive feedback** or praise lets employees know that their performance is on track.

- **Constructive feedback** provides direction when employees need to modify some aspect of their performance.

- **Corrective feedback** is appropriate when a performance problem has become more serious.

Whichever kind you give, be sure to handle each one separately, without swinging back and forth between criticism and praise.

When it comes to deciding which kind to give, keep this in mind: Not every employee will need corrective feedback. Often, constructive feedback is all an employee needs to improve performance. But every employee needs ongoing positive and constructive feedback. Why? Because almost every employee (unless he or she is about to be terminated) does something right. Always look at your employees' performance in terms of specific workplace behaviors—don't just label them "good" or "bad" employees. Encouraging positive behavior while helping employees correct problematic behavior is what feedback is all about.

"I always thought it was enough to just give employees thorough feedback during the appraisal meeting. But my new boss had different ideas. She was committed to the idea that managers should meet with their direct reports four times a year to give feedback. Even though I really wasn't convinced, I scheduled quarterly meetings with my employees. During the very first round of meetings, something happened that convinced me that my boss was right. One of my employees said she was glad I had scheduled the meeting because there was something that she needed to talk with me about, but she hadn't been able to find the right moment. She had a minor issue with the way her team leader was delegating work, and I realized that the semiformal nature of the meeting was just right for raising her concerns. She needed a private setting for this, but she wasn't comfortable scheduling a private meeting on her own. It would have made what she wanted to talk with me about too much of a big deal. But I also know that if she had waited until the end of the year, the problem would have grown bigger until it took on a life of its own. Now I always make sure to ask my employees to think ahead of time about anything they'd like to raise during the quarterly meetings."

Andreas B., Baltimore, MD

Tackle one topic at a time

Keep your feedback in focus

Very often, managers will try to save employees' feelings by sandwiching negative (constructive or corrective) feedback between two examples of positive feedback. This **sandwich approach** usually hinges on the use of the word "but" or "however." Here is how it usually goes: The manager starts out with an example of good performance, followed by "but . . ." and an example of not-so-good performance, and then ends with a positive comment. For example, "Sarah, you did a wonderful job clearing out the old inventory stock, but you didn't update the computer files like you did when you worked on inventory last year." This can have the unintended effect of undermining the constructive feedback you wished to give. Worse, it can also result in employees becoming hesitant to receive positive feedback from you for fear that it will always be followed by bad news.

So what should you, as manager, do instead? Address every topic separately, as you would do during the actual performance appraisal meeting. If you only deal with one topic at a time, you don't need to worry about transitioning from positive to negative, or vice versa. To take the example above, a better approach would be to praise the employee's inventory management talents when it's appropriate to do so. Then, if an issue about computer abilities or attention to detail comes up, make sure to let the employee know about it—right away.

ASK THE EXPERTS

I have to deliver some serious corrective feedback to an employee, but I don't want to end on a down note. How should I end the conversation?

Even though the "sandwich" approach to feedback should be avoided, ending corrective feedback sessions on a positive note is actually a very good idea. For example, you might say something like, "I think you've come up with a workable solution, and I have faith in you. I think you can turn this situation around, and I'm ready to support you as you do that." As long this employee is still employed by your organization, there is still hope that he or she can bring performance up to an acceptable level. This is especially true if you and your employee collaboratively develop a strategy for improving performance.

Just be careful that you don't allow this positive ending to become an unrealistically optimistic vision of the future. For example, if you know that an employee will never be your top performer, don't insinuate that this is possible by saying something like, "I know that with a little effort you can be our top employee!" In addition to being unrealistic, this is not a specific goal and lacks any strategy for achieving it. Stay grounded in reality—the most truthful version of reality toward which you and your employee can reasonably strive.

The feedback meeting

A step-by-step approach to holding regular performance discussions

A feedback session isn't a formal meeting—it's a discussion. One of the most important objectives of this discussion is that you and your employee leave with a shared understanding of where things stand in terms of the employee's performance relative to his or her goals.

The following step-by-step approach will help you and your employee reach that shared understanding:

Step 1: Present your assessment of the employee's performance—goal by goal and competency by competency.

Step 2: Invite the employee to respond.

Step 3: Discuss and reconcile any different perceptions the two of you might have.

Step 4: Support the employee in his or her efforts to identify ways to bring all dimensions of his or her performance up to standards.

Step 5: Collaborate to develop an action plan for moving forward.

Some managers are most familiar with the technique of discussing the areas in which employees performed well first, and then areas where performance was not as strong. This sandwich approach to feedback (see page 200) can backfire, however, and employees may not really hear the good news.

In organizations where feedback meetings are held regularly, managers are often required to fill in feedback forms that look much like appraisal forms (see page 17). Even if not, it might help to model your feedback on the sections of the appraisal form. In these cases, go through the feedback form in order, discussing the ways in which the employee has performed well, as well as the ways in which the employee didn't meet expectations, in whatever order they are listed. Give the employee a copy for his or her files, and put one into the employee's performance file.

CHOOSE THE SETTING CAREFULLY

Preparing the setting for a feedback meeting is a lot like preparing the setting for a performance appraisal meeting. The two most important considerations: where and when.

Where

■ Try to have the meeting where there won't be any interruptions—a conference room is ideal. If that isn't possible, use your office, and do what you can to minimize interruptions (see page 159).

■ It's best not to conduct feedback meetings on the phone, although sometimes this is unavoidable—especially if you must manage from a distance. If the decision comes down to not providing any feedback at all to having to provide it over the phone, do use the phone. But realize that you'll miss a lot of information that the employee might be communicating nonverbally (see page 164), and the meeting will be a lot less dynamic.

When:

■ In general, avoid Mondays and Fridays. These are often busy days, and employees (and even you) may be thinking more about the weekend than the workweek.

■ Avoid early mornings and late afternoons, which can also be busy times. You may be either gearing up for the current day or getting ready for the next one. Another problem with late afternoons is that employees may have postwork obligations, which can result in a distracted or rushed discussion.

■ As with the phone, however, sometimes you can't always pin down the ideal time or environment for giving feedback. Again, if the choice comes down to providing feedback in less than ideal circumstances or not providing any at all, go with what is possible right now.

Giving positive feedback

Because no news is not necessarily good news

Giving positive feedback, or praise, is an important but often over-looked part of the feedback process. Have you ever heard managers (or even yourself) express the following ideas?

- "No news is good news."
- "I'll let them know if there's a problem. Otherwise, it's status quo."
- "My employees know they're doing well and that I appreciate them."
- "I don't have time to give them praise regularly."
- "Since my company is not giving out any bonuses this year, I don't feel right telling people what a good job they have done."

Sometimes such managers end up not giving their employees any feedback—or even worse, giving only negative feedback. Feedback is vital, especially positive feedback. When giving out feedback, tell them you're going to give them positive feedback. Stick to one subject. And be brief—it should take a couple of minutes at most. Here are several ways to provide good feedback:

- Praise the employee's positive behavior, not the employee's personality or attitude. If you find yourself being overly general, look deeper to find behavior that supports what you're saying.

- Provide positive feedback quickly to reinforce the message and increase the likelihood that the employee will repeat the behavior.

- Provide detailed praise, because saying only "Great job!" does not really tell employees how they were effective.

- Discuss their positive performance with them. Ask them how they attained this high level of performance; this might be helpful info for other employees. Some may also want to share credit with coworkers.

- Describe how the employee's praiseworthy behavior contributes to the goals of the individual, the department, and the organization.

ASK THE EXPERTS

Is it true that employees should be "praised in public and criticized in private"?

Sometimes. The "criticize in private" part of that statement is usually true, but it's important to formulate this as constructive feedback, rather than personal criticism. The "praise in public" part, however, isn't true for everyone. Some people love being recognized in public. Others become extremely uncomfortable with public praise—so much so that they may try to avoid repeating the positive behavior that resulted in the praise. Instead of encouraging positive behavior, you could end up discouraging your employees from excelling.

Should I praise employees a certain number of times every day, or every week?

Praise doesn't follow a mathematical formula. Look for legitimate opportunities to provide positive feedback to your employees, but don't force it. Your employees will know if you do, and the praise will have no value. In fact, it's better to give no praise at all than to give forced, artificial, or dishonest praise. Try to "catch" employees doing something right, then praise them for it right away.

Giving constructive feedback

Help employees see this as an opportunity

When you give your employees feedback about specific ways in which they need to improve their performance, having a step-by-step plan will help you to be better prepared and to feel more confident. The following four-step approach provides a simple and straightforward way to give **constructive feedback**:

Step 1: Offer objective observation. Describe to your employee what you have seen, heard, and/or measured. Use objective and unemotional terms. Do not speculate or make assumptions about what the employee's underlying motives might have been. Also note that it sometimes helps to preface these observations with the words "You may not realize this." Why? Because it's the truth! People don't always realize what they are doing or understand the full impact of their behavior on others.

Step 2: Describe the impact of the behavior. Actions can be like a stone dropped into a pond, and can create a ripple effect throughout an organization. So be sure to let the employee know how his or her actions (or inactions) have impacted coworkers, organizational goals, customers, etc. Again, use objective and unemotional terms. Don't speculate about how others might have been impacted; stick to what is factual, and therefore not open to debate.

Step 3: Invite discussion. Ask the employee for his or her input and reactions. Initiate conversation and discussion. Ask open-ended questions, and encourage the employee to share his or her perspective.

Step 4: Collaboratively decide on next steps. Don't lay out a solution for your employee. Instead, brainstorm together. The two of you might come up with better ideas than either of you could come up with on your own. Be there to support your employee, not to rule with an iron fist. This will ultimately help you build trusting relationships with your employees.

CONSTRUCTIVE FEEDBACK SESSION

To make this four-step process a little more real, take a look at this example. You are the manager of your company's accounting department. Jake is an assistant manager in your shipping department. His job is to oversee the shipment of products to the oversees. Here are some ideas about how a manager could approach a constructive feedback discussion with Jake:

Step 1: "Jake, I'd like to talk with you. You may not realize this, but of the 2,500 shipping orders you handled last quarter, 75 of them were late. That's a 3% error rate. The acceptable standard is 1%."

Step 2: "This error rate resulted in a number of customer complaints, not to mention internal complaints from several departments that had to readjust their numbers because the late deliveries resulted in late payments."

Step 3: "I'd like to hear your thoughts on this, Jake. What's your take on your performance? How might you have done things differently to prevent these errors? Is there anything about the shipping procedures we have in place that is standing in your way of getting these shipments out on time?"

Step 4: "I think we both have a better understanding of the situation now. What ideas do you have about what you can do to bring your performance up to expectations? How can I support you in this?"

Giving corrective feedback

When an opportunity becomes a problem

Despite managers' best efforts to address performance concerns before they become performance problems, it can still happen. This is the point at which your approach should shift from constructive to corrective feedback. Essentially, **corrective feedback** is what is required when the employee has not brought his or her performance up to expected levels even after receiving constructive feedback from you. You don't want to corner the employee or badger the person, but your goal is to state the seriousness of the situation and to provide support. Here is a step-by-step approach:

Step 1: Make sure the employee was aware of performance expectations. Before the meeting, ask yourself whether the employee was fully aware of these, and confirm this in the meeting with the employee. If you have any doubts, consider whether it's really appropriate—and fair—to escalate from constructive feedback to corrective feedback at this time. When making that determination, take into consideration the nature of the behavior, as well its seriousness. Then consider whether you have already given the employee constructive feedback about the same behavior; if the answer is yes, then proceed with steps 2 and 3.

Step 2: Make sure the employee understands the seriousness of the situation. At the beginning of the meeting, make certain that the employee understands the gravity of the situation. No longer are the two of you discussing "opportunities for improvement"; rather, it is possible that the employee's continued employment may be in question if the performance problem continues.

Step 3: Make sure the employee doesn't feel there is "no way out." Try not to send a message of hopelessness—or helplessness—during the meeting. Yes, things are serious, but the employee can work through this, and you, the manager, are there to provide support. Striking this balance isn't always easy, but it becomes easier with practice.

ASK THE EXPERTS

Do I need to write anything down when I give corrective feedback, or can I just talk with the employee?

It's important to have written documentation of a corrective feedback meeting (in fact, documenting all meetings is a good idea; see pages 184–185). Also, know your organization's "progressive discipline" policy and follow through on it appropriately with respect to this situation. See pages 182–183.

Lead your team to success

One of the biggest challenges of providing useful feedback and managing for ongoing success is that both tasks require you to be a *manager*, not a teammate. Especially in cases where new managers are given the responsibility of managing their former peers, and where they are required to give constructive or corrective feedback, it can be difficult for these managers to create—and feel comfortable with—the authority they need to manage effectively.

As you build on the performance appraisal process by providing regular feedback, remember that being a manager is very different from being an individual contributor or team member. It's more like being a coach or an instructor, and often requires you to train or tutor employees to display the kinds of skills and reach the level of performance that you are seeking.

What can make this complicated is that the kind of coaching you need to do depends on the employee and the type of feedback and direction he or she requires. It can mean encouraging your stars, or top performers, to find new ways to keep performing well, or pushing your solid performers to live up to their potential. It can also mean helping to correct the poor performance of underachievers.

Managing effectively always means supporting employees and helping them reach their goals, but it never means doing their work for them. This fact is key if you want to take the insights you gained through the performance appraisal process and create year-round success by communicating clearly and often with employees.

All of this should be in the front of your mind as you strive to motivate employees to greater achievement. Your effective coaching will help employees perform well, which in turn will lead to positive evaluations at the end of the performance appraisal period—and will ensure that your workplace remains a harmonious, productive place to be.

ASK THE EXPERTS

I've been a manager for years but this is the first I've heard about being a coach to employees. I don't really know a thing about it. Where do I start?

There are books, consultants, software packages, and online classes that teach these skills to managers (see the resources at the end of this chapter), so find out what's available to you and what you are able to commit to, then do it! Part of being a good coach means finding out what you don't know—and then learning it—so there's nothing to really be anxious about. Think of it this way: When you were hired or promoted to manager, you didn't know everything you needed to know about being an effective manager, nor could you have been expected to. Most managers have at least one—if not more than one—area in which they need to develop their skills. For many managers, this skill is coaching, so you're not alone. By learning to be a good coach, you'll enhance your value to your organization, and you'll set a good example to your employees, as well.

Helpful resources

Tools you can use

BOOKS

The Art of Giving and Receiving Feedback (Ami How-To Series)
by Shirley Poertner,
and Karen Massetti Miller

Feedback Toolkit: 16 Tools for Better Communication in the Workplace
by Rick Maurer

Difficult Conversations: How to Discuss what Matters Most
by Douglas Stone, Bruce Patton, Sheila Heen, Roger Fisher

WEB SITES

Success Factors Workforce Performance Management
www.successfactors.com
Information about setting up and using an automated performance management system.

"Performance Feedback: Getting Past Avoidance in the Quest for Excellence"
www.azspe.org/azdesigns/ azdsgn6_99a.html
This article by Harriet Rifkin offers practical—and positive—guidance and insight for delivering feedback in organizations.

Glossary

360-degree performance appraisal A type of performance appraisal in which the manager seeks input about the employee's performance from customers, coworkers, direct reports, vendors, and others who worked with the employee during the performance measurement period. Also known as a multirater performance appraisal.

Anniversary date A type of performance review system in which reviews are scheduled based on the date the employee was hired or promoted into his or her current position.

"BASIC" feedback principles This is a set of principles to guide feedback sessions, in which feedback should be B (behavior-based), A (as soon as possible), S (specific), I (interactive), and C (consistent).

Behavioral characteristics Traits or characteristics that a successful employee must have to perform the job successfully. Instead of focusing on personality or attitude, these characteristics are defined in terms of actual, observable, or measurable behaviors.

"Benchmark" effect This is a rater error, made by a manager during a performance appraisal, in which the manager uses the rating that he or she has earned from his or her own manager as the benchmark against which all other employees' performances are measured.

Central tendency effect This is a rater error, made by a manager during a performance appraisal, in which the manager tends to rate all of his or her employees in the middle of the performance rating scale.

Common review This is a type of performance review system in which all employees in an organization receive their performance appraisals at the same time, regardless of when they were hired. If merit increases are linked to performance appraisals, they will usually be effective on the same date for all employees, as well.

Competencies Particular skills or abilities that employees in a certain job, unit, or organization must possess and demonstrate to perform well.

Constructive feedback This is the kind of feedback that a manager gives to an employee when he or she needs to modify or improve some aspect of performance.

Contrast effect This is a rater error, made by a manager during a performance appraisal, in which the manager compares employees against each other instead of comparing their work against performance standards.

Corrective feedback This is the kind of feedback that a manager gives to an employee when he or she has a serious performance problem that needs to be corrected.

Cycle time This quantitative performance measure, sometimes incorporated into goals, describes the length of time it takes to complete a specific—and usually recurring—task from start to finish.

Day-to-day consistency The trait practiced by managers who behave in a relatively consistent manner with direct reports on a day-to-day basis.

Development goals Skills or competencies that an employee develops through extra training, classes, mentoring arrangements, etc. They can enhance job performance and help the employee grow within his or her chosen field or within the organization, and are often included in an "employee development" section on the performance appraisal form.

Direct report An employee (sometimes called a "subordinate") who reports to a manager or someone with more seniority in an organization.

Dissimilarity effect This is a rater error, made by a manager during a performance appraisal, in which the manager evaluates an employee more harshly because the employee is unlike the manager in some way. Those dissimilarities can be related to almost anything, including gender, age, race, religion, hobbies, interests, marital status, and parental status.

End date The date by which an employee needs to attain a particular goal.

Final draft The final version of the performance appraisal that a manager generates after revisiting and revising the draft appraisal. This should reflect any relevant information gleaned from the employee's self-appraisal, as well as any corrections or clarifications.

First draft A rough draft of the performance appraisal that a manager writes after reviewing the employee performance file, feedback notes, and other relevant documents.

Goal setting The collaborative process by which you and your employees jointly develop individual performance goals for them that support and reinforce your departmental goals.

Goals Projects or assignments that an employee is expected to accomplish during the performance measurement period. Goals may relate to specific, ongoing responsibilities that are a regular part of the job, or may be based on particular assignments or "special projects" that will be accomplished during the performance measurement period. Also known as objectives.

Good faith and fair dealing This is a legal concept, implied in the employer-employee relationship, that asserts that every employment relationship, regardless of whether an actual contract was signed, promises fair treatment.

Halo effect This is a rater error, made by a manager during a performance appraisal, in which the manager allows one out-standing area of an employee's performance to unduly influence his or her overall evaluation.

Horns effect This is a rater error, made by a manager during a performance appraisal, in which the manager allows one negative dimension of an employee's performance to overshadow all others.

Job analysis The process organizations use to collect, examine, and assess information about the responsibilities and tasks of a position.

Job description A document that summarizes the responsibilities, deliverables, minimum requirements/qualifications, essential and nonessential functions, and working conditions of a particular job.

Knowledge This refers to a specific body of information that an employee needs to know and apply while performing the job. Also known as areas of knowledge.

Leniency effect This is a rater error, made by a manager during a performance appraisal, in which the manager rates all of his or her employees too generously, to be nice or to avoid conflict.

Mathematical approaches to rating systems These are two types of mathematical formulas that are used to calculate ratings for each section of the performance appraisal, or for the entire appraisal. Sometimes that formula is weighted—meaning that certain goals or competencies are rated as more important than others.

Measurements (or measures) Standards or levels of expected performance that are incorporated into goals. At the end of the appraisal period, measures are used to evaluate and assess the degree to which employees met their goals.

Mentor An employee who teaches or advises another employee. Mentoring can be done on a casual basis or via a formal program. Normally, more experienced employees will mentor less experienced ones.

Motivational factors The financial—and perhaps even more importantly, non-financial—reasons why employees are motivated to come to work every day. These can include a desire for fulfilling work, prestige, and status.

Nonmathematical approaches to ratings systems This type of ratings system, used on performance appraisal forms, does not provide a formula for calculating ratings. Instead, managers are asked to choose a phrase, such as "exceeds expectations," that reflects the employee's performance.

Objectives Projects or assignments that an employee is expected to accomplish during the performance measurement period. Goals may relate to specific, ongoing responsibilities that are a regular part of the job, or may be based on particular assignments or special projects that will be accomplished during the performance measurement period. Also known as goals.

Organizational consistency This is the type of consistency shown by an organization when all managers and all employees in all departments are treated the same.

Outputs These are the "end results" that an employee in a certain position is supposed to produce. In a manner of speaking, outputs define and describe why the position exists.

Performance appraisal meeting A formal discussion between a manager and an employee to review the employee's performance appraisal form, talk about and evaluate the employee's performance during the performance appraisal period, and begin planning performance objectives for the new appraisal period.

Performance measurement period This is the time frame during which a manager measures, assesses, and evaluates an employee's performance. Also called the "performance appraisal period."

Performance-related label On a performance appraisal form, this is a general phrase (such as "far exceeds expectations") that describes and rates an employee's specific behaviors or actions, as opposed to personality or attitude.

Person-related label On a performance appraisal form, this is a general term or phrase (such as "excellent") or a letter grade that describes or rates an employee's performance in terms of personality or attitude.

Person-to-person consistency This is the kind of consistency shown by a manager who treats all employees equally and does not "play favorites."

Positive feedback (or praise) This is the positive information that a manager imparts to an employee to confirm that the employee's performance is on track.

Progressive discipline This is a series of steps that managers take to address performance concerns. In some organizations, this includes verbal warnings, written warnings, possibly suspension, and termination.

Quality measures These are the standards used to evaluate whether a job's outcomes meet the requirements of quality.

Quantity measures These are the standards used to evaluate whether a job's outcomes meet the requirements of quantity, or amount.

Quarterly performance discussion (QPD) A meeting that a manager holds with an employee every three months to revisit the employee's objectives and progress toward reaching them.

Rater error An error in evaluation made by managers during performance appraisals.

Recency effect This is a rater error, made by a manager during a performance appraisal, in which a manager pays too much attention to employee performance near the end of the performance measure-

215

ment period instead of focusing on how the employee performed and behaved throughout the year.

Reciprocal appraisal An appraisal system in which employees have the opportunity to provide feedback to managers, with the aim of providing information that will help rectify employee concerns.

Reflective listening This is a management technique in which managers reiterate what an employee has said in their own words. It's effective for confirming the meanings, as well as feelings, behind what someone is saying.

Sandwich approach to feedback An unproductive practice in which a manager tries to cushion constructive or corrective feedback by "sandwiching" it between two examples of positive feedback.

Section A cluster of similar items—such as "goals" or "competencies"—on a performance appraisal form.

Self-appraisal An appraisal technique in which the employee evaluates his or her own performance by completing the same, or a similar, form that the manager will use to appraise him or her.

Similarity or "just like me" effect This is a rater error in which a manager evaluates an employee more generously because he or she shares something in common with the manager. These similarities can be related to gender, age, race, religion, hobbies, interests, marital status, parental status, and more.

Skills The specific abilities that an employee must posses and demonstrate in order to perform the job successfully. These can include technical, sales, administrative, or management skills, to name a few.

"SMART" An approach to writing goals that ensures that they fulfill the five following requirements: They must be specific, measurable, action-oriented, realistic, and time-bound.

Strictness effect A rater error in which a manager rates all of his or her employees too strictly.

Success rate A performance measure that specifies the degree to which specific standards of quality are attained by an employee. See also Measure.

Succession plan A plan for the future drawn up by organizations to anticipate—and make sure they can fill—staffing and leadership needs in the long term.

Suspension When an employee is asked by management to take leave from his or her job, with or without pay, for a defined period of time because of substandard performance.

Unit cost A measure that specifies what it costs to produce one unit (for example, a bar of soap) or to complete one processing cycle (for example, to process one mortgage application).

Upward appraisal A type of appraisal system in which employees evaluate their managers relative to specific expectations and behaviors.

Verbal warning A conversation in which a manager informs an employee that his or her performance does not meet performance expectations, and gives the employee a chance improve. In some progressive discipline systems, an employee can be terminated after a set number of verbal warnings.

Volume A quantity measure, often used when setting performance goals, that specifies how many of a product must be made or completed.

Written warning This is a memo or letter, written by a manager, that documents and describes areas in which an employee's performance does not meet standards, and outlines next steps if performance is not brought up to standards.

Index

About the author

Cathy Lee Gibson is the Director of Human Resources Management Programs at the Metropolitan Office of Cornell University's School of Industrial and Labor Relations in New York City. She has over 15 years of management experience in the field of Human Resources, and has coauthored online workshops entitled "Performance Management and Appraisal," "Managing Performance," "Effective Interviewing," and "Fundamentals of Compensation." She earned a BA degree, summa cum laude, from Ithaca College and a MA in Business Administration from Pace University, where she was recognized for outstanding scholarship in the field of management.

Barnes & Noble would like to thank the following consultants for their help in preparing this book: **Scott Cohen**, Ph.D., National Practice Leader for Talent Management, Watson Wyatt Worldwide, in Boston, MA; **Rosanna Goni**, Director of Customer Intelligence of Belmay, Inc., in Yonkers, NY; and **Jim Seese**, Director of Human Resources at Wink, Inc., in New Orleans, LA.

Barnes & Noble Management Basics™

Barbara J. Morgan Publisher

Barb Chintz Editorial Director, Barnes & Noble Basics

Leonard Vigliarolo Design Director

Wynn Madrigal Senior Editor

Emily Seese Editorial Assistant

Della R. Mancuso Production Manager

Illustrations by Barton Stabler/ARTVILLE